Authentic Recipes in an Instant Pot™

The Latest Way to Cook British Food

Geoff Wells

Authentic English Recipes
Book 12

Cover Artwork & Design by
Old Geezer Designs

Published in the United States by
Authentic English Recipes
an imprint of
DataIsland Software LLC,
Hollywood, Florida

https://ebooks.geezerguides.com

ISBN-13: 978-1981675029

ISBN-10: 1981675027

Table of Contents

ENTRÉES

HOTPOTS

INSTANT POT RICE

CURRIES

STEAMED PUDDINGS

DESSERTS

APPENDIX

DEDICATION

This series of books are dedicated to Mildred Ellen Wells 1906 - 2008

Mom lived for 102 incredible years. She went from horse drawn carriages and sailing ships to bullet trains and moon rockets.

She was not a fancy cook but everything she made tasted great. My dad grew much of what we ate in our garden so everything was always fresh and free of chemicals.

This book is a collection of some of her best recipes. I have just translated the quantities for the North American market.

I know she would be delighted to see all her recipes collected together so that you can continue to make these great tasting dishes.

Geoff Wells - Ontario, Canada - September 2012

INTRODUCTION

I get really ticked off when I hear disparaging comments from people about British food, particularly people that eat at McDonald's and spray cheese from a can. Obviously they have never eaten a real Authentic English Recipe.

I will admit that most of what we eat is not very fancy, we tend to cook mostly plain, good tasting, satisfying food. This series brings you a selection of downright delicious food that we Brits have been eating for hundreds of years.

It's great to try new recipes for the first time. To experience new flavors and food combinations you may never have thought of. But for most of our day to day cooking we never open a cookbook or precisely measure ingredients. We go by what feels right and the experience of having cooked the same meal many times before.

The "How To Make Authentic English Recipes" series is more about the method and the ingredients than it is about precise measuring.

Don't worry, I'll give you lots of measurements, (imperial and metric) so you'll get perfect results the first time. But after awhile you'll learn how to "wing it" and create great meals from fresh ingredients rather than packages.

This is the way our Grandmothers cooked and these are recipes my Grandmother passed down to my mother and she passed down to me.

I have changed these recipes so they work in the Instant Pot. Same great taste but easier and quicker to make

I hope you enjoy the series and will soon be cooking like a true Brit.

BREAKFAST

The *Full English Breakfast* is world famous and a must have for any tourist. It's not hard to put everything together yourself, particularly when you have all the directions that you will find in the sixth book of this series "How To Make English Breakfast With Bubble & Squeak & Homemade Baked Beans"

https://ebooks.geezerguides.com/how-to-make-english-breakfast-with-bubble-squeak-homemade-baked-beans/

The full breakfast, kippers, and porridge are about all the traditional breakfast meals I can think of. These days most people have toast & tea or sugary cereal.

Traditional English-Style Baked Beans (No-soak method)

A tomato-based style of baked beans is generally the traditional type served with an English Breakfast. This Instant Pot no-soak recipe makes it easy to have Traditional English baked beans quickly - although I strongly recommend that you keep your beans a day before serving. The sauce will thicken and the flavours will mature.

Ingredients

- 2 tablespoons (30 mL) olive oil
- 1 medium onion, chopped
- 2 cloves garlic, minced
- 1 small carrot, peeled and finely chopped
- 1 stalk celery, finely chopped
- 2 cups (450g) dried white navy beans
- 2 cups (480 mL) vegetable broth or water
- 4 cups (900g) canned diced tomatoes
- 2 tablespoons (30 mL) Worcestershire sauce
- 3 tablespoons (45 mL) tomato paste
- 1 teaspoon (5 mL) balsamic vinegar
- 1 tablespoon (15 mL) dark brown sugar
- 2 teaspoons (10 mL) sea salt
- 1 bay leaf

Method

1. Select Sauté mode and allow the inner pot of your Instant Pot to heat up.
2. Add the olive oil and allow it to heat up.
3. Add the onion, garlic, carrot and celery and sauté for 3-4 minutes.
4. Press Cancel to turn off Sauté mode.
5. Add the rest of the ingredients and stir well.
6. Close and lock the lid, ensuring the Pressure Valve is in the Sealing position.

7. Select the Bean/Chili Function and set the cooking time for 25 minutes.

8. When cooking time is complete, allow a full Natural Pressure Release. This means waiting until the Float Valve drops on its own.

Tip: this can take up to 45 minutes.

Tip: You can simply turn off your Instant Pot - press Cancel - and wait for the Float Valve to drop or you can let it go into Keep Warm mode, which it should do automatically. In Keep Warm mode the time will start counting up, ie you'll see L0:00, L0:01, L0:02, etc. It's counting up the minutes since the Bean/ Chili function completed.)

9. Once the Float Valve has dropped, carefully open the lid, remove the bay leaf and give everything a good stir.

10. It may seem like there's a lot of liquid, but the beans will continue to absorb the sauce even after it has cooled down, so don't be tempted to thicken it.

Tip: The bake beans will taste much better if you let them sit for a day, allowing the flavors to mature. So, package them up and let them sit in the fridge for a day. You can have them cold or warm them up. Whatever your preference is.

POACHED EGGS

The Instant Pot method for poached eggs takes a lot of the guesswork out of the equation and the eggs never actually get immersed in the water.

INGREDIENTS

2-4 eggs (depending on how many servings you want)
1 cup (240 mL) water

METHOD

1. Place the water in the inner liner of your Instant Pot.

2. Spray individual silicone cups (one for each egg) with a non-stick cooking spray.

3. Crack one egg into each of the silicone cups and carefully place the cups on a stainless steel or silicone trivet.

4. Gently lower the trivet into the Instant Pot.

5. Close and lock the lid ensuring the Pressure Valve is in the Sealing position.

6. Select Steam mode and set the cooking time for 3 or 4 minutes.

    (We find we get a perfect poached egg at 3 minutes but your preference may vary. If you like a solid yolk, select 5 minutes.)

7. When the cooking time is complete, do a Quick Release to release all of the pressure.

8. Once all of the pressure is released, carefully open and remove the lid and gently lift the trivet out of the Instant Pot.

9. Carefully slide the poached eggs out of the silicone cups onto a toasted English muffin and enjoy!

Plain Steel Cut Oats

This breakfast staple, popular in England, Scotland and Wales, can be easily dressed up with a splash of cream and some seasonal fresh fruit, such as fresh-picked blackberries.

As a matter of fact, while vacationing on a narrowboat, we simply pulled the boat to the side of the canal where there were plentiful wild blackberries and picked enough for breakfast. They were so ripe that our fingers were purple by the time we were done picking.

Ingredients

1 cup (80g) steel cut oats
2 cups (475 mL) water
⅛ teaspoon (0.625 mL) sea salt

Garnish

Garnish with cream, fresh fruit and sugar, if desired.

Method (Pot in Pot)

1. Place one cup (240 mL) of water into Instant Pot inner liner and place a trivet in the pot.

2. In a heatproof bowl, that fits into the inner liner, combine the steel cut oats, water and salt.

3. Place the dish on the trivet. Cover if you prefer, but it is not necessary.

4. Close and lock the lid ensuring the Pressure Valve is in the Sealing position.

5. Select the Porridge function and set the cooking time for 6 minutes.

6. Once cooking time is complete, allow a Natural Pressure Release for 5-10 minutes and then release the rest of the pressure by carefully turning the Pressure Valve from Sealing to Venting.

7. Once all of the pressure has been released and the Float Valve has dropped, carefully remove the lid.

8. Carefully remove the dish with the cooked oats and serve immediately.

9. Garnish as desired.

SERVINGS: 3-4

Almond Buckwheat Porridge

This hearty breakfast is sugar-free, the sweetness is provided by the chopped prunes.

Ingredients

1 cup (250g) buckwheat groats
2 cups (475 mL) whole milk
2 cups (475 mL) water
¼ cup (40g) raisins
¼ cup (30g) prunes, chopped and packed
1 teaspoon (5 mL) vanilla
¼ cup (20g) chopped almonds

Method

1. Rinse the buckwheat groats well and place them in the Instant Pot.

2. Add all the other ingredients and stir well.

3. Close and lock the lid and ensure that the valve is in the Sealing position.

4. Select Manual/Pressure Cook and set the cooking time for 6 minutes.

5. When the cooking time is complete allow a Natural Pressure Release (can take up to 20 minutes).

6. Once the pressure is completely released, carefully remove the lid, stir the porridge and serve.

APPLE AND SPICE STEEL CUT OATS

This is possibly the closest you can come to the taste of apple pie for breakfast.

INGREDIENTS

> ½ cup (40g) steel cut oats
> 1 large apple, cored and chopped
> 1½ cups (360 mL) water
> 1½ (7.5 mL) teaspoons cinnamon
> ¼ teaspoon (1.25 mL) allspice (can substitute ground cloves)
> ¼ teaspoon (1.25 mL) nutmeg
> 1 tablespoon (15 mL) maple syrup or honey

METHOD

1. Add all items to the Instant Pot except the Maple Syrup and stir well.

2. Close and lock the lid, ensuring that the Pressure Valve is in the Sealing position.

3. Select Manual/Pressure Cook and set the cooking time for 3 minutes.

4. Once cooking time is complete and allow a Natural Pressure Release.

5. Once pressure has been fully released, carefully open and remove the lid.

6. Stir in the maple syrup or honey and serve.

AFTERNOON TEA

Devon is one of my favorite areas in England. If I was to go back to live I would most likely choose Devon.

It is the South of England and enjoys the best climate with warm summer days and gentle sea breezes.

The coast is dotted with quaint fishing villages that have changed little in hundreds of years.

After a day of sightseeing by the time 4pm rolls around you'll probably be ready for a spot of tea. So it's good that the tea shops are so easy to find. Just squeeze yourself into one of the little tables and order a Devonshire Tea.

Devonshire tea is not a tea blend like Earl Grey or Orange Pekoe, it is a ritual performed everyday in small tea rooms throughout Southern England and particularly the County of Devon. A favorite pastime for both locals and tourists this tradition should definitely be on your to-do list whenever you visit Devon.

Real English tea with milk, fresh hot scones with homemade strawberry jam and mounds of clotted cream are what is on the menu at 4 o'clock in the afternoon.

This is an occasional indulgence so don't stress over the calories - just enjoy it.

Strawberry Jam

Making strawberry jam in your Instant Pot is a little easier than making it the traditional way. It requires less stirring and is less messy because it eliminates those inevitable splatters that occur when using a stove-top method.

Ingredients

2 pounds (900g) strawberries, cleaned, stemmed and roughly chopped

2½ cups (500g) granulated sugar

4 tablespoons (60 mL) lemon juice, preferably fresh

Method

1. Place all the ingredients in the Instant Pot and select the Sauté mode. Mix well and continue stirring until all the sugar has melted.

2. Turn off Sauté mode and place the lid on the Instant Pot. Turn the Pressure Valve to Sealing.

3. Select Manual/Pressure Cook and set for 6 minutes. When time is up, use a Natural Pressure Release.

4. Once the pressure is released, remove the lid and stir the jam.

5. If you want a less chunky jam, mash the strawberries using a potato masher. (optional)

6. Select the Sauté mode and allow the strawberries to cook for approximately 10 minutes. It should start to feel thicker.

7. Carefully spoon the jam into sterilized Mason jars while still warm and seal the jars "finger tight". Allow to cool on a wooden cutting board. The metal lids should seal as the jam cools. If any do not seal properly, use them first.

The jam should keep in the refrigerator for 2 to 3 months or in the freezer for 6 months.

CLOTTED CREAM

Clotted cream is a must with Devonshire Tea but can be rather fiddly and time-consuming to make.

This Instant Pot recipe makes it much easier to achieve amazing results so that you can, indeed, have an authentic Devonshire Tea experience.

INGREDIENTS

4 cups (950 mL) heavy cream (whipping cream)
Note: DO NOT purchase ultra-pasteurized cream as it won't work.

METHOD

1. Pour the cream into Instant Pot insert, close and lock the lid ensuring the Pressure Valve is set to Sealing.

2. Set Instant Pot mode to Yogurt Boil. To achieve this, press the Yogurt button and then the Adjust button until you see the word "Boil".

3. When the Instant Pot beeps, indicating that the boil setting is done, press the Keep Warm button. The Keep Warm mode maintains the temperature between 145°F and 172°F (63°C to 78°C).

4. Leave on the Keep Warm setting for 8 hours.

5. Turn off your Instant Pot, remove the lid and remove the insert. Place the insert on a wire rack to cool. Be careful not to agitate the cream too much. Agitating will cause the cream to mix back into the milk liquids underneath, reducing the amount of clotted cream you end up with.

6. Allow the cream to cool for about an hour at room temperature.

7. Cover the pot with plastic wrap and put in the fridge for at least 8 hours, again, being careful not to agitate the cream.

8. After 8 to 12 hours the clotted cream will have thickened.

9. Using a slotted spoon, gently skim the thick layer of clotted cream from the surface, leaving the whey behind, and ladle into a jar or bowl. Sterilized Mason jars would work well.

10. This recipe will yield about 2 cups (480 mL), perhaps a little more, of clotted cream.

If you like your clotted cream to be a little less thick, stir some of the whey back into it.

DON'T throw the whey out! You can use it to make Whey Scones.

Refrigerate the clotted cream and use within 4-5 days.

Also refrigerate the whey and use it up within 4-5 days as well. You can substitute whey for buttermilk in any recipe that calls for buttermilk.

Bonus Recipe: Whey Scones

After you've made your clotted cream, you won't want to waste the whey. This recipe makes lovely, fluffy scones and uses the leftover whey.

However, if you don't have any whey, you can always substitute buttermilk or regular whole milk.

Ingredients

2 cups (240g) all-purpose unbleached white flour
4 teaspoons (20 mL) baking powder
2 tablespoons (30g) cold butter
1 cup (250 mL) Whey

Method

1. Pre-heat the oven to 425°F (220°C, Gas Mark 7).

2. In a large bowl, combine the flour and baking powder. Mix well.

3. Using a pastry blender, or two knives, cut in the cold butter until the mixture resembles breadcrumbs or a coarse oatmeal.

4. Add the whey, mixing just enough to combine.

5. Turn the mixture out onto a lightly floured surface and gently knead to form a smooth dough.

6. With the palms of your hands, press the dough out to a thickness of about ½ inch (1.25 cm) overall.

7. Use a 2 to 2½ inch (5 to 6.3 cm) round cookie cutter to cut the scones out of the dough.

8. You can re-use any scraps left over from cutting the dough by reforming and cutting again. Note: Only do this once. After that the dough will become too tough and too dry.

9. Gently place the scones, close together but not touching, on a lightly greased baking sheet.

10. Brush each scone with a little whey (or milk).

11. Bake at 425°F (220°C, Gas Mark 7) for 12 to 15 minutes or until golden brown.
12. Remove from the oven and allow to cool on a wire rack.

SOUPS & STEWS

The Instant Pot is possibly the most versatile cooking appliance you own. It excels at so many tasks it is sometimes difficult to decide which recipes to cook the traditional way and which to cook in the Instant Pot. Some people have solved this dilemma by purchasing more than one.

One thing, I believe most people will agree, is that preparing soups and stews is the Instant Pot's greatest strength.

Once you learn which ingredients go well together it's fairly easy to make original soups from whatever you have available. Many years ago I made an original soup that my wife, Vicky took into work for lunch. She got quite a few questions about it as I had labeled it, *Cream of Fridge*. It was made from an assortment of compatible leftovers so the name seemed to be appropriate.

STOCK

A soup or stew, in the most basic terms, is water flavored with meat and/or vegetables. But, if you just throw everything into a pot and boil it, you're not likely to get the results you were hoping for.

Good, hearty, flavorful soups and stews are simple to make but very few people, in my experience, seem to be able to get it right.

For the best results, you should always start with stock rather than plain water. On their own, for most of your soups and stews, the meat and vegetables you use won't provide enough flavor to plain water.

Any time you boil your vegetables, a lot of the goodness and flavor ends up in the water you throw away. If you plan to use it in a day or two, save any of the water you use to boil potatoes, carrots, cabbage, etc. and put it in the fridge to use as stock.

Another option is to buy a can or tetra pack of broth. You can get beef, chicken and vegetable broth at most grocery stores. This will give your soups an excellent start but most of the commercial broths contain a lot of salt and other unwanted chemicals.

It's a good idea to make your own stock from soup bones however, today we don't often see soup bones in the supermarket. When I was younger, my mother would get soup bones from our local butcher, but real butchers are something else you don't often see anymore.

I should qualify that last statement that I'm talking about the USA. England still has real butcher shops and many Canadian supermarkets still have butchers on staff that can supply bones and even kidney or suet if you ask. I don't know, but I imagine Australia and New Zealand are much the same.

In other words, if you're reading this in the USA, you're most likely going to have to use a can of broth.

Wait, before you write nasty reviews complaining about my comments on American food I want to point out that things are getting better. The good food movement is gaining popularity with the availability of fresh local produce and cooking family meals from scratch rather than from a package has never been more popular. It's a good start, let's hope it continues.

I got a little sidetracked with the bones. I was talking about making stock.

Ham stock

If you buy a ham shoulder they usually have a large bone in the middle that you end up throwing away. Don't. Put the bone in a heavy pot, big enough to hold it, cover it with water and simmer it for an hour or two.

Remove the bone and give it to your (or your neighbor's) dog. Put the pot in the fridge (after it has cooled). When it is well chilled, remove the fat that has hardened on the top of the jelly. Yes, I said jelly. Don't worry, it will liquefy as soon as you warm it up.

Turkey stock

Have you ever weighed your turkey leftovers? I'm not talking about the half dozen plastic wrapped packages in the freezer you are saving for sandwiches. I'm talking about the skin, bones and giblets you throw in the garbage when you cook a whole turkey.

You might be surprised that it is almost 50% of the weight of your original turkey. But don't throw it all out. You can use it to make the most marvelous stock for your stews and soups.

Do the same as you did with the ham bone. Put everything in a big, heavy pot - the skin, bones, giblets, leftover stuffing, any jelly off the carving plate - all of it. Cover with water and simmer for a couple of hours. Let it cool then strain the resulting stock into a bowl.

First, use a slotted spoon to lift out the largest pieces of bone, then pour what's left through a sieve to catch all the small bones and pieces of turkey that have now been cooked to death.

Throw this whole mess in the garbage and get it out to the curb as soon as possible because in a couple of days it's really gonna stink.

Just to be clear, any good pieces of meat should not go into the stock pot - reserve those for later to go into your turkey soup.

VEGETABLE STOCK

OK, now forget everything I just said about saving vegetable water and boiling bones - you have an Instant Pot - so there is a better way.

You probably throw away a fair bit of vegetable matter. The thick stalks of broccoli, outside cabbage leaves, carrot peelings etc. All kinds of flavourful skins and cut off ends that are not parts you want to serve. Instead of throwing it all in the garbage, put it in a plastic bag in your freezer. When you have collected a bag full you can make some Instant Pot Stock.

Here's the type of vegetable peelings and bits you should save:

- carrot peelings and ends
- celery leaves and ends
- potato peelings
- yam (sweet potato) peelings
- outer bits of onions (not the yellow part, but the tough outer white layer)
- garlic (the end you cut off before mincing, not the papery stuff)
- apple cores
- lettuce leaves that have wilted (iceberg, romaine, etc)
- summer squash and zucchini ends
- mushroom stems
- pea pods

Add the following sparingly because of their somewhat overwhelming flavor and odor.

- cabbage leaves
- broccoli stems
- cauliflower cores

I use a one-gallon Ziploc™ Freezer Bag (approximately 10" x 10" - 25 cm x 25 cm) to collect my peelings and make broth once it is full (not packed).

INGREDIENTS

1 bag of saved frozen vegetable peelings and bits
12 cups (2.8 L) water, approximately*
*Don't add water above the fill line

METHOD

1. Place the water and the contents of the bag in the Instant Pot's inner pot.

2. Close and lock the lid, ensuring that the Pressure Valve is in the Sealing position.

3. Select Soup mode and set the cooking time for 90 minutes.

4. Once cooking time is complete, allow a complete Natural Pressure Release. That means just turning the Instant Pot off and waiting for the Float Valve to drop on its own.

5. Once the pressure has completely released, carefully open and remove the lid.

6. Carefully, using oven gloves (mitts are too clumsy), remove the inner pot to a heatproof surface and allow to cool.

7. Using a slotted spoon, remove all the large pieces of the vegetables.

   (Tip: You can put this in your compost or blend it with some water and feed it to your plants. They love it!)

8. Then strain the rest of the liquid through a fine sieve and discard any additional vegetable matter (as mentioned above).

9. Place the vegetable broth in containers and freeze for later use.

   (Tip: Measure the amount of broth you put in each container. You can put frozen vegetable broth directly into an Instant Pot recipe and now you know how much you are adding.)

Beef/Ham Broth

It's just as easy to make a beef/ham broth as vegetable stock, using soup bones you got from your butcher (see the discussion under Stock on page 17)

Even supermarkets without a butcher on staff will occasionally sell cut up soup bones in the foam trays.

Ingredients

beef soup bones that will fit in the pot
12 cups (2.8 L) water, approximately*
*Don't add water above the fill line

Tip: to get the most flavor out of the bones, you may want to roast them a little first. To do that, pre-heat the oven to 450°F (230°C, Gas Mark 8), place the bones on a rimmed baking pan and roast for 20 minutes, turning once at the 10 minute mark. Then, proceed with the rest of the recipe as directed.

Method

1. Place water and bones in the Instant Pot inner pot.

2. Close and lock the lid, ensuring that the Pressure Valve is in the Sealing position.

3. Select Soup mode and set the cooking time for 90 minutes.

4. Once cooking time is complete, allow a complete Natural Pressure Release. That means just turning the Instant Pot off and waiting for the Float Valve to drop on its own.

5. Once the pressure has completely released, carefully open and remove the lid.

6. Carefully, using oven gloves (mitts are too clumsy), remove the inner pot to a heatproof surface and allow to cool.

7. Using a slotted spoon, remove all the bones

   (Tip: There won't be much left in the way of nutrition in the bones but I'm sure your dog will love to chew it just the same.)

8. Place the broth in containers and freeze for later use.

TURKEY BROTH

Do you remember the line in Jurassic Park, "just because you can, it doesn't mean you should." That probably applies to making turkey broth in the Instant Pot.

If you just cooked up a breast or a drumstick then by all means use the left over bones and skin to make a rich base for a chicken or turkey soup like I described above.

It's more a question of size than anything else. There is just so much left over from the average family turkey, (50% waste) that it takes 3 or 4 cycles of the Instant Pot to accommodate it all. *See the <u>Stock</u> discussion on page 17 for more detail*

If you decide to go ahead divide your leftovers into piles that will fit in the pot.

INGREDIENTS

bones, skin, leftover stuffing, bits of meat, jelly
12 cups (2.8 L) water, approximately*
Don't add water above the fill line

METHOD

1. Place the water and turkey leftovers in the Instant Pot's inner pot.

2. Close and lock the lid, ensuring that the Pressure Valve is in the Sealing position.

3. Select Soup mode and set the cooking time for 90 minutes.

4. Once cooking time is complete, allow a complete Natural Pressure Release. That means just turning the Instant Pot off and waiting for the Float Valve to drop on its own.

5. Once the pressure has completely released, carefully open and remove the lid.

6. Carefully, using oven gloves (mitts are too clumsy), remove the inner pot to a heatproof surface and allow to cool.

7. Using a slotted spoon, remove as much of the bones and skin as you can.

   (Tip: Get this out to the garbage as soon as you can because the hot meat will spoil quickly)

8. Then strain the rest of the liquid through a fine sieve and discard any additional material as above.

9. Put the strained liquid in the fridge to chill so that you can remove any fat. The chilled fat will float to the top and harden, making it easy to remove.

GREASE

I'm not telling you to remove the fat for health reasons - although that is a very good reason - you just don't want your soup or stew to have a greasy taste.

It's always a good idea to put a handful of rice in any stew that is potentially greasy - particularly chicken and turkey.

How to Make a Perfect
Scratch Soup/Stew Every Time
Beef - Chicken - Lamb - Vegetable - Ham - Turkey

Before I present any specific recipes I would like to go over a few general suggestions for making scratch soups and stews. To be honest these are the ones you are likely to make the most often.

Beef bourguignon, mulligatawny, minestrone, gazpacho, and other named soups have specific ingredients and an expectation of a particular taste. Scratch soups and stews are the ones you put together yourself, that hopefully taste good, but will unlikely ever be made exactly the same again.

They will always taste good because you know what ingredients go well together, which spices to use, how long to cook them and how to rescue your mistakes.

This section is about how to "wing it" and make a great meal in your Instant Pot without any particular recipe.

Here are a few rules you need to apply to pretty much any soup or stew.

Rule #1 Don't Use Too Much Water

You use water to dilute so many things, doesn't it make sense that if you add a lot of water to your soup/stew you will dilute the flavor. Of course, you should try to start with a stock rather than water. *See the earlier notes on stock -page 17.*

Rule #2 Make Your Stew at Least a Day Before You Plan to Serve It

You want to give your soup/stew's flavor the opportunity to develop. You also want the soup/stew to cool so you can remove any fat from the surface. This is particularly important when you are making ham, chicken or turkey stew, which can be especially greasy.

Rule #3 Use Premium Ingredients

I suppose it's tempting to try to get rid of all the leftovers in the fridge by making a stew out of them. But that won't make a stew you will be proud of. A piece of stringy celery, a lump of fat or meat you can't chew can spoil even the best tasting dinner.

Rule #4 Taste It Before You Serve It

Don't be as surprised as everyone else if your stew doesn't taste right. There are ways to fix most disasters. So, before you throw it out and call for take-out, read on.

See "When It All Goes Pear Shaped", later in the book.

Rule #5 For Instant Pot Users

Although not absolutely essential, it is a good idea to use the "Meat/Stew" setting. By choosing this setting your stew will cook at the ideal levels of temperature and pressure.

Because, with the Instant Pot, vegetables do not need to be immersed in water to cook, you can use much less stock and make a stew with a more intense flavour.

Vegetables

You can put almost any vegetable you like into your soup/stew and the resulting flavor will change either slightly or significantly - depending on how strong a flavor the vegetable has and how much you use.

As a minimum, I always like to start with carrots and onions. Next would be celery, potatoes and a little bit of cabbage.

I like peppers in a salad but in a stew they can take over the flavor if you use too much. The same is true for celery root.

Zucchini is okay but does not add much flavor and goes mushy if cooked too long. It's best to add any soft vegetables like this during the last few minutes before the stew is done. If you are using the Instant Pot add them after pressure cooking and do a few minutes on sauté.

If you are one of those people who will only eat the very top of broccoli, then a stew is a great way to use the stalks you would otherwise throw away. Just keep the stalks in a plastic bag in the freezer until you need them. Don't go crazy with this veggie, though. Up to a half-inch (1.25 cm) thick piece of stalk is fine. Leave it in bite size pieces or chop it up, either way it makes a great addition to your stew.

You see what I mean about winging it. Use quality ingredients and some common sense. Put in what you like and it will be fine.

Spices

With a few exceptions, I don't add many spices. My wife likes to add a couple of bay leaves (particularly to a ham stew) but, personally, I don't think they make much difference.

I usually add a couple of shakes of Worcestershire sauce and a bouillon cube, which we'll talk about in a minute.

The exception is turkey stew, which, in my opinion, is greatly improved with sage. If you stuff your turkey with a sage and onion stuffing, and some of the leftover stuffing makes it into the stock, then you will get some of the flavor. But, be sure to taste it to see if you need to add some more.

Bouillon

A watery stew may still be full of goodness but it doesn't taste very good. Kick your taste up a notch or two by adding a bouillon cube or liquid towards the end of the cooking process.

My favorites, in order, are Bovril™, OXO™ and Knorr™. I think you can get them in most grocery stores in the Western world although in the USA you may have to look in the imported foods section.

You can also get store brands and bouillon cubes from the dollar store, but watch out for the salt content. Some of these imitations are so salty they can ruin your meal.

When using your Instant Pot it's OK to add liquid bouillon before you close the lid but be careful of cubes and powders. Sometimes they will clog the vent so you should add them after you remove the lid.

SALT

I often add a teaspoonful (5 mL) or two to a 3 quart (2.85 L) saucepan of soup/stew. It really helps to bring out the flavor - but taste it before and after. Add just a little at a time. You can always add more salt, if needed, but you can't take it out.

And, watch out for the cheap bouillon cubes. Try spooning out some of your stew into a measuring cup and dissolving your cube in that before adding it to the pot. This way, if it is super-salty, you can toss it down the sink without ruining all your hard work.

SOUP OR STEW

Sometimes the line between soup and stew seems to blur and you're not really sure at what point your soup has become a stew.

I think a soup has a base liquid with a predominate taste, such as tomato or onion, and little or no other additions. Then, of course, you can have Tomato Vegetable or French Onion, (with bread and grated cheese).

A stew has a less identifiable base flavour and lots of additions such as meat and vegetables.

Given these qualifiers I'll leave the scratch soups to your experiments and just give you some recipes for particular soups.

Scratch stews are easy, quick and tasty. Just follow the following guidelines.

THE PROCESS

OK, I think you have enough background, it's time to put it all together and make a stew.

If you're making a red meat stew from scratch you start with the meat but I'm including my "Perfect Every Time Beef Stew Recipe" at the end of this chapter so for now we'll cover stews from leftovers.

Since the ham, chicken or turkey is already cooked, it gets added right at the end because all you want to do is warm it up.

We've already talked about how important the stock is, but if you don't have any you can use water and some extra bouillon.

PREPARE YOUR VEGETABLES

At a minimum, you'll need a medium to large yellow onion and 3 or 4 carrots. If you can find carrots that still have their green tops, that's best, otherwise you will have to settle for the ones in the poly bag. Just make sure they are reasonably fresh and break with a snap. If you cut the carrots in wheels their flavor tends to get lost. I prefer 1 to 2 inch (2.5 to 5 cm) pieces so that when you eat them you get the full carrot taste. The same goes for the onions, if you finely chop them you will flavor the stew water but you won't get the same taste experience that you do from a decent bite-size piece.

You might want to consider keeping all your vegetables to bite-size so that each mouthful has its own distinct taste.

Celery is another great addition to a scratch stew and a few potatoes should always go into a poultry stew to help soak up any potential grease.

LEFTOVER STEW

If you skipped over the section, "How to Make a Perfect Scratch Stew Every Time", please go back and read it. (see page 25)

What is leftover stew, you ask?

It's a way to use up whatever is left over from the Sunday roast.

Basically you make a vegetable stew then, as a last step, you add the leftover meat and turn off the heat.

Just be conscious of what you're adding to your stew. The quality of the meat should not be any less than what you served as the Sunday roast. Don't ruin your hard work by using scraps that should be given to the dog. Trim off the fat and gristle. If it's tough, putting it in the stew won't improve it.

INGREDIENTS

1 tablespoon (15 mL) olive oil
1 large onion coarsely chopped
4 medium carrots cut in half lengthwise then in 2 inch (5 cm) pieces
2 stalks celery cut into 1 inch (2.5 cm) chunks
2 potatoes chopped in ½ inch (1.25 cm) pieces
broth (vegetable, beef or turkey) to cover, approximately 3-4 cups (700-950 mL)
2 tablespoons (30 mL) bouillon (vegetable, beef or poultry)
Leftover cooked meat of your choice, cut into bite-size pieces, approximately 2 cups (300g)
Salt and pepper to taste

METHOD

1. Select Sauté mode and allow the inner liner of your Instant Pot to heat up.

2. Add the olive oil and allow it to heat up.

3. Add the onions and sauté for 2-3 minutes.

4. Press Cancel to turn off Sauté mode.

5. Add the rest of the ingredients, with the exception of the cooked meat.

6. Close and lock the lid ensuring the Pressure Valve is in the Sealing position.

7. Select Manual/Pressure Cook mode and set the cooking time for 4 minutes.

   Tip: this seems like a short time but, remember, at this point we're only really cooking the vegetables and we want them to be cooked but still firm.

8. When the cooking time is complete, allow about a 5 minute Natural Pressure Release (just so you don't get broth spewing out of the valve) and then release the rest of the pressure by carefully turning the Pressure Valve from Sealing to Venting.

9. Once all of the pressure has been released and the Float Valve has dropped, carefully remove the lid.

10. Select Sauté mode and bring the liquid to a low simmer.

11. Add salt and pepper to taste.

12. If you find that the stew needs thickening, mixed together about a tablespoon (15 mL) of cornstarch with just enough water to make a pourable paste.

13. Slowly drizzle the cornstarch into the simmering liquid, stirring constantly until the desired consistency is reached.

14. If you plan to add dumplings now would be the time.

15. Press Cancel to turn off Sauté mode.

16. Add the leftover meat and allow it to heat through - about 5 minutes.

17. Serve immediately, or cool and refrigerate to allow the flavors to blend, then reheat before serving.

Yellow Split Peas

Yellow split peas go very well with ham and will add lots of flavor and body to your soup or stew. The only problem is that they take a long time to cook. If you put them in with the other ingredients, they will still be like little bullets when your carrots are just right. If you cook them long enough so that they soften then your potato chunks will have disappeared into the liquid.

The solution, of course, is to make them part of the stock and cook them long enough to be incorporated into the stock. You can hurry the process along a bit by using a blender to smooth out your stock.

Fortunately, now that you own an Instant Pot, you can add the split peas directly to you soups and stews for their distinct flavour and thickening ability. So long as you are cooking under pressure for at least 6 to 10 minutes everything should be fine. But please, no more than about ¼ cup (55g), as they swell up quite a bit and could take over your stew.

Pease Pudding

Growing up our next door neighbour would occasionally make and share some pease pudding. I considered this a treat and ate it, as is, with a spoon. I don't know why, but it was not something my mother made.

OK, this has nothing to do with making stews, it's more about the split peas - so consider it a bonus.

You can use split peas to make an interesting substitute for your usual rice or potatoes. All you do is boil them long enough to absorb all the water you are cooking them in.

Ingredients

  1⅓ cups (300g) dried split peas, yellow or green
  water to soak split peas
  2 tablespoons (30 mL) olive oil
  1 medium yellow onion, diced
  1 small carrot, diced
  2 cups (475 mL) vegetable broth, preferably homemade or water (see page 17 Stock)
  1 teaspoon (5 mL) sea salt
  ½ teaspoon (2.5 mL) black pepper, freshly ground

 Add to cooked peas
  2 tablespoons (30g) butter
  2 large eggs

Method

1. Soak the split peas for 30 minutes in approximately 2 cups of water (enough to cover by and inch (2.5 cm) or so).

2. Drain and set aside.

3. Select Sauté mode and allow the inner liner of your Instant Pot to heat up.

4. Add the olive oil and allow it to heat up.

5. Add the onions and carrots and sauté for 2-3 minutes.

6. Add the split peas and give them a quick stir.

7. Press Cancel to turn off Sauté mode.

8. Add the broth, salt and pepper and stir well.

9. Close and lock the lid ensuring the Pressure Valve is in the Sealing position.

10. Select Bean/Chili mode and set the cooking time for 10 minutes.

11. When the cooking time is complete, allow a full Natural Pressure Release. That means allowing the Float Valve to drop on its own. This can take 20-30 minutes.

12. Once all of the pressure has been released and the Float Valve has dropped, carefully remove the lid.

13. If you haven't already, press Cancel to turn off your Instant Pot.

14. Remove the inner liner to a heatproof surface and give the peas a quick mash with a potato masher. Then beat in the butter and the eggs.

15. Pour into a greased 2 pint (950 mL) pudding basin. (Make sure it fits in your Instant Pot.)

16. Cover the basin with greaseproof paper or a double layer of aluminum foil, greased on the side it will come in contact with the pease pudding.

17. Then cover with a pudding cloth. Tie the pudding cloth securely in place with some twine and gather the edges of the cloth and tie on top. (This will make it easier to remove from your Instant Pot.)

Finish cooking your pudding

1. Thoroughly wash out the inner liner of your Instant Pot so you can use it again.

2. Place a trivet in the inner liner of your Instant Pot.

3. Place the pudding basin on top of the trivet.

4. Add enough water to come about ½ of the way up the pudding basin.

   Tip: In our 6-quart Instant Pot that was about 6 cups or 1.4 L.

5. Close and lock the lid ensuring the Pressure Valve is in the Sealing position.

6. Select Steam mode and set the cooking time for 10 minutes.

7. When the cooking time is complete, allow a complete Natural Pressure Release. That means allowing the Float Valve to drop on its own. This can take 20-30 minutes.

8. Once all of the pressure is released and the Float Valve has dropped, carefully remove the lid.

9. Then, carefully remove the pudding and place on a wire rack or heatproof surface.

10. Carefully remove the coverings and invert the pudding onto a serving dish.

11. Cut into slices and serve immediately.

SERVES: 4–6

Best Beef Stew Ever

The Instant Pot excels at stew and with this recipe you will be sure to make the best beef stew you have ever tasted.

I am about to share a family recipe that is over one hundred years old. I hope that you will try it exactly as I present it, at least once. If not, you will be missing one of your life's most amazing taste experiences.

Quite a build-up but for many years after I left home I jokingly accused my mother of not sharing the magic ingredients as I was unable to reproduce the flavor I had grown up with.

Turns out it is not so much the ingredients as the process, which is what I have tried to stress in this book.

Ingredients

3 pounds (1.5 Kg) blade or top sirloin roast, cut into ¾ - 1 inch (2 - 2.5 cm) cubes
1 large onion, cut in bite size pieces
3 - 4 large carrots, cut into 1 inch (2.5 cm) pieces
1 tablespoon (15 mL) Bovril™
1 teaspoon (5 mL) salt, or to taste
Stock to cover
3 ounces (85g) beef kidney, cut into 6 pieces (optional but recommended)
2 teaspoons (10 mL) cornstarch (or sufficient)

The Beef

There's an old saying about not making a silk purse out of a sow's ear. The same principle applies here. Your finished stew will only be as good as your ingredients and your major ingredient is the beef.

You can generally find shrink-wrapped trays of "stewing beef" in your local supermarket - avoid them. Take a look at some of the inexpensive roasts. Blade or top sirloin roasts are often cheaper per pound than "stewing beef" and will make a much better stew. Get something around 3 - 4 pounds (1.4 - 1.8 Kg). This will make 4 - 6 meals, more if you don't eat much.

Cut the roast into cubes about ¾ - 1 inch ((2 - 2.5 cm) on each side. Remember, they will shrink quite a bit when cooked. Make sure you remove any fat, gristle, etc. and watch out for string. Butchers love to tie roasts up in string and it's not very tasty.

KIDNEY

The Brits said OK, the Americans said Yuck, Canadians and Australians are probably divided.

Americans can use the excuse that kidney is almost impossible to find in any supermarket. You will need to go to one of the premium chains, like AJ's, and order it specially.

If you're not willing to try it, you are really missing out. If there is a secret ingredient in this recipe - this is it.

One beef kidney is enough to make 5 or 6 stews.

You don't have to eat it but you do need it to flavor the rich gravy. My wife is Canadian and loves the flavor but even after more than thirty years together she still won't eat any kidney.

Cut the kidney into 5 or 6 pieces and individually wrap and freeze what you don't need. Cut the piece you will use into smaller pieces and remove the strip of fat in the middle.

If you don't plan to eat it, you can leave it in larger chunks, which will make it easier to identify and remove.

METHOD

1. Dust the beef and kidney with unbleached all purpose flour.
2. Press the Sauté key on the Instant Pot and add the beef and kidney to the stainless steel inner pot, stirring vigorously to prevent the meat from sticking.
3. When the meat is seared, pour in just enough stock to cover the meat.

Both the meat and the vegetables have water content, which they lose during cooking. The meat will shrink and you will end up with more liquid than you thought.

4. Add the carrots, onions, Bovril™ and salt.

5. Close and lock the lid ensuring the Pressure Valve is set to Sealing.

6. Click the Meat/Stew button and set the cooking time to 20 minutes.

7. When the cooking time is complete allow a total Natural Pressure Release. This means allowing the Float Valve to drop on its own.

8. Carefully open and remove the lid. Mix the cornstarch with just enough water to make it liquid and stir it into the stew. If the stew doesn't thicken you may have to turn on Sauté for a few minutes to bring to a simmer while stirring.

9. Taste it to see if you need more salt or Bovril™.

   You can remove the kidney now, if you are not going to eat it. Your dog or cat will just love it.

10. You can serve it right away but the flavours will mature if you leave it until tomorrow.

How Thick?

How thick should the gravy be? This is something that is so easy to do but difficult to write about. All I can think of is that it should be about the consistency of motor oil. Not a very appetizing analogy but at least you get the idea. Growing up, my daughter used to call it chocolate gravy.

Let The Flavors Mature

Pour the cooled stew into a container and put in the fridge overnight. Next day, heat the stew and add dumplings if you wish. Serve with mashed potatoes and fresh peas.

Steak And Kidney Pie

If you really want a treat, you can combine this stew recipe with my wife Vicky's pastry recipe for a steak and kidney pie that will have your guests begging for more. See her book "Perfect Pastry Every Time by Vicky Wells" on Amazon.

Cock-a-Leekie Soup

Cock-a-Leekie soup is considered the national soup of Scotland. However it's current name did not come into general use until some time in the 18th Century.

Ingredients

3 slices thick-cut bacon, chopped

1 tablespoon (15g) butter

3 leeks, white and light-green part, sliced into rings (Tip: Be sure to wash the leeks thoroughly. They can be quite sandy.)

1 stalk celery, sliced

1 carrot, halved lengthwise and sliced

2 cloves garlic, minced

6 pitted prunes, chopped

2-3 large boneless, skinless chicken breasts, cut into ½-inch (1.25 cm) cubes

1 large bay leaf

¼ teaspoon (1.25 mL) black pepper, freshly ground

2 teaspoons (10 mL) thyme

1 teaspoon (5 mL) marjoram

½ teaspoon (2.5 mL) red pepper flakes

1 tablespoon (15 mL) apple cider vinegar

⅔ cup (135g) pearl barley

10 cups (2.4 L) chicken broth, preferably homemade (see page 17 - Stock)

Method

1. Select Sauté mode on your Instant Pot and allow it to heat up.

2. Sauté the bacon for a minute or so then add the butter, leeks, celery, carrot, and garlic.

3. Stir well and add a little of the broth to deglaze the bottom of the pot, using a wooden or silicone spatula to scrape up and loosen any browned bits from the bottom of the pan.

4. Press the Cancel button to turn off Sauté mode.

5. Add the prunes, cubed chicken breasts, spices, cider vinegar, barley, and chicken broth.

6. Close and lock the lid, ensuring the Pressure Valve is in the Sealing position.

7. Select Soup mode and set the cooking time to 12 minutes.

8. When cooking time is complete, do a Quick Release.

9. Once all the pressure has been released and the Float Valve has dropped, carefully open and remove the lid.

10. Season with salt and pepper as desired.

Mulligatawny Soup

It sounds like it should be Irish but then you discover it contains curry so now you think it's Indian. Well that's sort of right but mulligatawny is actually an English soup based on a Tamil recipe. Look it up on Wikipedia.

INGREDIENTS

¼ cup (60g) butter
2 pounds (900g) raw boneless, skinless chicken breast, cut into bite size pieces
1½ teaspoons (7.5 mL) sea salt, divided
1 teaspoon (5 mL) black pepper, freshly ground, divided
1 cup (150g) yellow onion, diced
1 cup (100g) celery, diced
1 cup (175g) sweet bell pepper, diced
1 cup (150g) carrots, diced
3 cloves garlic, minced
¼ cup (50g) lentils
¼ cup (55g) basmati rice
⅛ teaspoon (0.625 mL) ground cloves
⅛ teaspoon (0.625 mL) nutmeg, freshly grated
2 teaspoons (10 mL) curry powder, divided
4 cups (950 mL) chicken stock, preferably homemade (see page 17 - Stock)
1 cup (118g) apple, chopped (I prefer to leave the skin on)
¼ cup (5g) cilantro, chopped
1 tablespoon (15 mL) lemon juice, fresh squeezed if possible
1 cup (240 mL) heavy whipping cream
freshly chopped cilantro for garnish, optional

METHOD

1. Select Sauté mode and allow it to heat up.
2. Add the butter and allow it to melt and become a bit bubbly.

3. Add the chicken and sauté until lightly browned.

4. Season with ½ teaspoon (2.5 mL) salt and ½ teaspoon (2.5 mL) freshly ground black pepper.

5. Remove the chicken and set aside.

6. Add the onions, celery, peppers, carrots, garlic, lentils, rice, nutmeg and 1 teaspoon (5 mL) of the curry powder to the pot.

7. Season with 1 teaspoon (5 mL) salt and ½ teaspoon (2.5 mL) freshly ground black pepper and stir well.

8. Press the Cancel button to turn off Sauté mode.

9. Add the chicken stock and stir, using a wooden or silicone spatula to scrape any bits off the bottom of the pot.

10. Place a steamer basket on top of the ingredients and place the browned chicken in the steamer basket.

11. Close and lock the lid, ensuring the Pressure Valve is in the Sealing position.

12. Select the Soup function and set the cooking time for 18 minutes.

13. When cooking time is complete, turn the Instant Pot off and use a Quick Release.

14. Once all of the pressure has been released and the Float Valve has dropped, carefully remove the lid, take out the steamer basket with the chicken in it and set aside.

15. Press the Sauté button and add the apples and 1 teaspoon (5 mL) of curry powder (or to taste) and add salt, to taste.

16. Bring the mixture to a simmer, stirring occasionally.

17. Loosely place the lid back on (the warning "Lid" may flash - or you can use a separate sauce pan lid) and leave for 3 to 5 minutes until the apples are soft.

18. Once the apples are soft, use an immersion blender to blend the soup to a smooth consistency.

19. Return the chicken back to the pot and add the lemon juice, cilantro and cream.

20. Stir well and serve.

Vegetarian Mulligatawny Soup

Ingredients

1 tablespoon (15 mL) extra virgin olive oil
2 carrots, peeled and roughly chopped
2 onions, roughly chopped
1 stalk of celery, roughly chopped
3 slices of fresh ginger (about quarter size) peeled
5 cloves of garlic, roughly chopped
2 tablespoons (30 mL) curry powder
1 teaspoon (5 mL) ground coriander
6 cups vegetable broth, homemade if possible
1 medium baking potato, scrubbed but unpeeled, roughly chopped
¾ cup coconut milk
2 tablespoons (30 mL) lime juice, fresh if possible
3 tablespoons fresh cilantro, chopped (optional)

Method

1. Select the Sauté mode and allow the inner liner to heat up slightly.

2. Add the olive oil, carrots, onions, celery, ginger and garlic and sauté for 2-3 minutes.

3. Add the curry and coriander and sauté for another minute.

4. Add the vegetable broth and stir.

5. Add the chopped potato and stir.

6. Close and lock the lid of the Instant Pot ensuring that the Pressure Valve is in the Sealing position.

7. Select the Soup mode and set the cooking time for 18 minutes.

8. Once cooking time is complete, allow a Natural Pressure Release for 10 minutes and then manually release the rest of the pressure.

9. Carefully unlock and remove the lid.

10. Carefully remove the inner liner to a heatproof surface.

11. Using an immersion blender, blend the soup until smooth, then add the coconut milk and lime juice and stir well.

12. Serve immediately, using the chopped cilantro as a garnish, if desired.

13. This soup also freezes well.

Potato Leek Soup

Potato leek soup is rich and creamy with a mild flavor, perfect for a cool day with a slice of warm, crusty bread.

Ingredients

3 tablespoons (45 mL) olive oil

4 large leeks, white and light green parts only, roughly chopped (Tip: Be sure to wash the leeks thoroughly. They can be quite sandy.)

3 cloves garlic, minced

2 pounds (900g) Yukon Gold potatoes, roughly chopped into ½-inch (1.25 cm) pieces (you can peel them if you prefer, I didn't)

7 cups (1.6 L) chicken or vegetable broth, preferably homemade (see page 17 - Stock)

2 bay leaves

½ teaspoon (2.5 mL) dried thyme leaves

1 teaspoon (5 mL) salt

¼ teaspoon (1.25 mL) black pepper, freshly ground

1 cup (240 mL) heavy cream

Chives, finely chopped, for serving, optional

Method

1. Select Sauté mode and allow the inner liner of your Instant Pot to heat up.

2. Add the olive oil and allow it to heat up.

3. Add the leeks and garlic and sauté for 2-3 minutes.

4. Press the Cancel button to turn off Sauté mode.

5. Add the stock and use a wooden or silicone spatula to scrape any bits from the bottom of the pan.

6. Add the potatoes, bay leaves, thyme leaves, salt and pepper.

7. Stir well.

8. Close and lock the lid, ensuring that the Pressure Valve is in the Sealing position.

9. Select Soup mode and set the cooking time for 10 minutes.

10. When cooking time is complete, allow a Natural Pressure Release for 10 minutes, press the Cancel button to turn off the Instant Pot and then release the rest of the pressure by carefully turning the Pressure Valve to the Venting position.

11. Once the pressure has been completely released, and the Float Valve has dropped, carefully open and remove the lid.

12. Using an immersion blender, blend the soup until it is mostly smooth.

13. Add the heavy cream and stir well.

14. If the soup has cooled too much, Select the Sauté mode and bring it back to a simmer. Then press the Cancel button to turn off the Sauté mode.

15. Serve immediately.

Oxtail Soup

It's getting harder and harder to find Oxtails at any butchers. Once considered a "poor man's" meal, it is popular in many cultures. If you can find oxtails, you'll also find that it can now be quite expensive. But it's worth it for the lovely flavor and aroma this soup has.

Ingredients

5 pounds (2.2 Kg) oxtails
2 teaspoons (10 mL) sea salt
1 teaspoon (5 mL) black pepper, freshly ground
½ teaspoon (2.5 mL) nutmeg, grated
1 tablespoon (15 mL) olive oil
1 large yellow onion, chopped
3 large carrots, chopped
3 stalks celery, chopped
1 clove garlic, minced
2 cups (475 mL) red wine
1 cup (240 mL) beef broth, preferably homemade
(see page 17 - Stock)
2 whole cloves
2 bay leaves
1 cup (200g) fresh tomatoes, chopped
sea salt and fresh ground black pepper to taste

Method

1. In a large bowl, season the oxtails with the salt, pepper and nutmeg, tossing to make sure the salt and pepper is well distributed.

2. Select Sauté mode and allow the inner pot to heat up.

3. Add the olive oil and let it heat up.

4. Lightly brown the seasoned oxtails in the olive oil, a couple at a time, then remove from pot and set aside.

5. Add the onion, carrots, celery and garlic and sauté for 2-3 minutes.

6. Add a little of the red wine and bring it to a simmer. Use a wooden or silicone spatula to scrape any bits and deglaze the bottom of the pan.

7. Push the Cancel button to turn off Sauté mode.

8. Place the oxtails in the pot and add the rest of the wine, the beef broth, the whole cloves, the bay leaves and the chopped tomatoes. Stir well.

9. Close and lock the lid, ensuring that the Pressure Valve is in the Sealing position.

10. Select the Meat/Stew mode and set a cooking time of 40 minutes.

11. When cooking time is complete, press the Cancel button and allow a total Natural Pressure Release. That means waiting for the Float Valve to drop on its own.

12. When the Float Valve has dropped, carefully open and remove the lid.

13. Season the soup with salt and pepper to taste.

Guinness Beef Stew

According to Wikipedia "Guinness is an Irish dry stout that originated in the brewery of Arthur Guinness (1725–1803) at St. James's Gate brewery in the capital city of Dublin, Ireland."

Using Guinness makes for a flavorful stew and be sure to get enough so that the cook can have a pint or two as well.

Ingredients

2 pounds (900g) boneless beef roast (bottom round, rump, chuck)
Coarse salt and freshly-ground black pepper
3 tablespoons (45 mL) olive oil, divided
½ cup (30g) all purpose flour, divided
1 large yellow onion, chopped
12 ounces (350 mL) Guinness stout beer, divided (or substitute a stout beer of your choice)
2 to 3 garlic cloves, minced
6-ounce (120g) can tomato paste
1 tablespoon (15 mL) granulated sugar
1 tablespoon (15 mL) Worcestershire sauce
1 tablespoon (15 mL) dried thyme
1 teaspoon (5 mL) white pepper
2 dried bay leaves
8 cups (1.9 L) beef broth, preferably homemade (see page 17 - Stock)
1 teaspoon (5 mL) beef bouillon granules
5 to 6 large potatoes (such as Yukon Gold), cut into 1-inch (2.5 cm) cubes
4 to 5 carrots, peeled and cut into 1-inch (2.5 cm) chunks
3 to 4 celery stalks, cut into 1-inch (2.5 cm) chunks
1 leek, white part only, chopped

METHOD

1. Remove any excess fat from the beef roast and cut it into 1-inch (2.5 cm) cubes.

2. Select Sauté mode on the Instant Pot and press the Adjust button once so the display goes from Normal to More (Note: Some models don't have an Adjust button. If that is the case, press the Sauté button twice and the display should show More.)

3. When the screen displays "Hot", add half of the olive oil to the inner pot and allow it to heat up.

4. While the olive oil is heating, pat the beef cubes dry with paper towels. Don't skip this step because moist meat won't brown well.

5. In a medium bowl, season the beef cubes with salt and pepper and dust them with ¼ cup (30g) flour. Toss well until the beef cubes are well coated.

6. Brown the beef cubes in small batches and set aside.

7. Add the remaining olive oil to the inner pot and allow it to heat up again.

8. Add onions and sauté for a couple of minutes or until translucent.

9. Add 6 ounces (175 mL) of Guinness beer to the onions in the pot.

10. Bring the mixture to a boil and deglaze the bottom of the pot, using a wooden or silicone spatula to scrape up and loosen any browned bits from the bottom of the pan.

11. Add the tomato paste, garlic, sugar, Worcestershire sauce, thyme, white pepper, and bay leaves.

12. Stir well and press the Cancel button to turn off Sauté mode.

13. Add the browned beef cubes, the rest of the Guinness beer, the beef stock and beef bouillon.

14. Ensure that the inner pot is no more than ⅔ full and that all the ingredients are covered by the liquid.

15. Stir well to combine.

16. Close and lock the lid, ensuring the Pressure Valve is in the Sealing position.

17. Select the Meat/Stew function and set the cooking time for 20 minutes.

    Tip: If you have not changed the factory presets, you can select the Meat/Stew function and then press the Adjust button twice and a 20 minute cooking time should be selected. If your Instant Pot doesn't have an Adjust button, press the Meat/Stew button twice more to select the 20 minute cooking time. Otherwise, just push the "+" or "-" buttons to set the required cooking time.)

18. When the cooking time is complete, allow a Natural Pressure Release for at least 15 minutes.

19. Turn the Pressure Valve to Venting to release any remaining pressure and, when the Float Valve has dropped, carefully open and remove the lid.

20. Add the potatoes, carrots, celery and leeks and stir to combine.

21. Close and lock the lid, ensuring that the Pressure Valve is, once again, in the Sealing position.

22. Select the Manual/Pressure Cook function and set the cooking time to 10 minutes.

23. When the cooking time is complete do a Quick Release by carefully turning the Pressure Valve to the Venting position.

24. Once all the pressure has been released and the Float Valve has dropped, carefully open and remove the lid.

25. Add salt and pepper to taste.

26. If the stew requires thickening, create a thin paste by combining, in a small bowl, approximately 1 tablespoon (15 mL) of cornstarch and enough water to create a pourable paste.

27. Select the Sauté button and allow the stew to come to a simmer.
28. Stir in the cornstarch mixture, a little at a time, until the desired thickness has been achieved.
29. Press Cancel to Turn off Sauté mode.
30. Remove the bay leaves.

Tip: I always recommend that you make any stew a day ahead, giving time for the flavors to blend and mature. You can also use this stew as the filling for a Beef Pie or a Beef Suet Pudding. It can also be frozen for later use.

GUINNESS LAMB STEW

Guinness not only adds flavor to a stew, it also works like a tenderizer.

INGREDIENTS

3 pounds (1.4 Kg) lamb shoulder, well-trimmed and cut into 1½-inch pieces

3 tablespoons (45 mL) olive oil

2 teaspoons (10 mL) sea salt

1 teaspoon (5 mL) black pepper, freshly ground

¼ cup (30g) all-purpose flour

2 medium yellow onions, coarsely chopped

1 cup (240 mL) Guinness, divided (or substitute a stout beer of your choice)

3 tablespoons (45 mL) tomato paste

6 garlic cloves, minced

1 bay leaf

1 small sprig fresh rosemary

2 teaspoons (10 mL) sugar

5 cups beef or vegetable broth, preferably homemade (see page 17 - Stock)

4 large carrots, cut into 1-inch (2.5 cm) chunks

1 pound (454g) small white potatoes, cut in half

1 cup (150g) frozen green peas

METHOD

1. Remove any excess fat from the lamb shoulder and cut it into 1½ inch (4 cm) cubes.

2. Select Sauté mode on the Instant Pot and press the Adjust button once so the display goes from Normal to More (Note: Some models don't have an Adjust button. If that is the case, press the Sauté button twice and the display should show More.)

3. When the screen displays "Hot", add half of the olive oil to the inner pot and allow it to heat up.

4. While the olive oil is heating up, pat the lamb cubes dry with paper towels. Don't skip this step because moist meat won't brown well.

5. In a medium bowl, season the lamb cubes with salt and pepper and dust them with ¼ cup (30g) flour. Toss well until the lamb cubes are well coated.

6. Brown the lamb cubes in small batches and set aside.

7. Add the remaining olive oil to the inner pot and allow it to heat up again.

8. Add the onions and sauté for a couple of minutes.

9. Add half of the Guinness beer to the onions in the pot.

10. Bring the mixture to a boil and deglaze the bottom of the pot, using a wooden or silicone spatula scrape up and loosen any browned bits from the bottom of the pan.

11. Add the tomato paste, garlic, bay leaf, rosemary and sugar.

12. Stir well and turn off Sauté mode.

13. Add the browned lamb cubes, the rest of the Guinness beer and the beef or vegetable stock.

14. Ensure that the inner pot is no more than ⅔ full and that all the ingredients are covered by the liquid.

15. Stir well to combine.

16. Close and lock the lid, ensuring the Pressure Valve is in the Sealing position.

17. Select the Meat/Stew function and set the cooking time for 35 minutes.

    Tip: If you have not changed the factory presets, you can select the Meat/Stew function and it will default to a 35 minute cooking time. Otherwise, just push the "+" or "-" buttons to set the required cooking time.)

18. When the cooking time is complete, allow a complete Natural Pressure Release. This means allowing the Float Valve to drop on its own without touching the Pressure Valve.

19. Once all of the pressure has released the Float Valve has dropped, carefully open and remove the lid.

20. Add the potatoes and carrots and stir to combine.

21. Close and lock the lid, ensuring that the Pressure Valve is, once again, in the Sealing position.

22. Select the Manual/Pressure Cook function and set the cooking time to 10 minutes.

23. When the cooking time is complete do a Quick Release by carefully turning the Pressure Valve to the Venting position.

24. Once all the pressure has been released and the Float Valve has dropped, carefully open and remove the lid.

25. Add the frozen peas and salt and pepper to taste.

26. If the stew requires thickening, create a thin paste by combining, in a small bowl, approximately 1 tablespoon (15 mL) of cornstarch and enough water to create a pourable paste.

27. Select the Sauté button and allow the stew to come to simmer.

28. Stir in the cornstarch mixture, a little at a time, until the desired thickness has been achieved.

29. Remove the bay leaves.

Tip: I always recommend that you make any stew a day ahead, giving time for the flavors to blend and mature. You can also use this stew as the filling for a Lamb Pie or a Lamb Suet Pudding. It can also be frozen for later use.

WHEN IT ALL GOES PEAR-SHAPED

If you have used quality ingredients and followed my recommendations, there is not much that could go wrong. I can see just a few possibilities - too thick, too thin, too salty, or no taste.

Too Thick

If it's too thick then you've added too much cornstarch. Maybe you added the mixture when your stew was not quite hot enough and didn't realize you had added too much until the stew reached the right temperature and solidified.

No problem. Just stir in more liquid. Don't use water if you can avoid it because you will dilute the flavor. Use broth if you have it or make up some bouillon in a measuring cup and add that.

Too Thin

If it's too thin just mix up some additional cornstarch and slowly add it to the simmering liquid. Your stew must be almost boiling for the cornstarch to work. It's a chemical process and that's what it takes to activate the cornstarch molecules.

No Taste

If you used a good stock and quality bouillon, then taste should not be a problem. Just add more broth and bouillon.

If all else fails, put everything in a blender and make it into a creamy soup.

No, I'm not patronizing - I've done it. Sometimes that's just how you learn.

Too Salty

Too salty is tricky. Adding rice and potatoes will help to absorb the salt but the only way to dilute the taste, if it can't be rescued with rice or potatoes, is to make a second stew with absolutely no salt and mix the two together.

A Word About Dumplings

I love dumplings but an ever-increasing waistline has forced me to forgo this pleasure. They are easy to make and are a tasty addition to your stews. You add them to your stew just before you serve so don't make them and put them in the fridge overnight.

You can use suet, flour and baking powder but I like the results I get by using Bisquick™. Again I believe this name brand product is available from most grocery stores in the Western world and there is a dumpling recipe on the box.

In the Instant Pot you should add your dumplings after cooking your stew and use the sauté function to keep the stew simmering. Of course, you should not put the lid on while using sauté.

Dumplings also need to be covered for all, or most, of the time they are cooking. So, you're going to need a lid for your Instant Pot other than the regular, locking lid.

Tip: It doesn't need to be a tight fitting lid, so you can probably find a lid from one of your regular pots and pans that will work. I like to use a glass lid from one of my other saucepans when I do dumplings for one of my Instant Pot stews. With a glass lid I can keep an eye on them.

Note: If you are not going to serve your Instant Pot stew right away, you can always reheat the stew in a regular saucepan, bring it to a simmer and do the dumplings then.

Suet Dumplings

Dumplings are a lovely additional to any hearty stew and, yes, you can add them to a stew cooked in your Instant Pot, too.

However, you only want to add dumplings to a stew that you are going to serve immediately.

Ingredients

½ cup (120g) flour
¼ cup (30g) shredded <u>suet</u> (<u>see page 140 for alternatives</u>)
¾ teaspoon (3.75 mL) baking powder
⅛ teaspoon (1.25 mL) salt
5 tablespoons (75 mL) cold water, approximately

Method

1. Put the flour, suet, baking powder and salt in a small bowl and mix well. Add just enough cold water to make the dough pliable but not sticky.

2. If it's too sticky add a little more flour.

3. Put a little flour on your hands and divide the dough into 8 pieces then roll them into balls.

4. After your stew is cooked and you have removed the Instant Pot lid click the Sauté button to keep your stew simmering.

5. Drop the dumpling balls into the simmering liquid. Keep covered and cook gently until done, (about 10 - 15 minutes). Turn them over half way through the process.

Regular Flour Dumplings

Ingredients

2 cups (240g) all-purpose flour
1½ teaspoons (7.5 mL) salt
1 tablespoon (15 mL) baking powder
2 tablespoons (30 mL) olive oil
1 cup (240 mL) warm water

Method

1. In a medium bowl, combine the flour, salt and baking powder. Mix well.

2. Add the oil and water and mix until you achieve a smooth batter.

3. Dumplings are meant to be soft but not too sticky, so add a little more flour or water as necessary.

4. Drop by large spoonfuls into a simmering stew and cook, covered for 10 - 15 minutes or until they are cooked through.

   Tip: If you like, you can add some finely chopped herbs (parsley, basil, etc.) to the dumplings batter.

ENTRÉES

The Instant Pot is a wonderfully versatile appliance and most users are still exploring its capabilities. It cooks quickly, it tenderizes and it requires negligible supervision. But, it's not the best choice for everything. Really good cuts of meat, for example, are best when traditionally roasted.

In this book I concentrate on what the Instant Pot does best not just on what it can do.

The entrée section is short but leads into Hot Pots and Curries, plus be sure to check out the savoury steamed puddings at the end of the Steamed Puddings section.

Instant Pot Roasting

Although cooking your Sunday roast in a pressure cooker may not really seem like "roasting", it still produces an amazing tender and tasty roast.

Technically, roasting is a dry heat process so it is wrong to call cooking in the Instant Pot roasting but it definitely gets the job done and in a very short time.

Not only that, because you need to have some liquid in the pressure cooker for the pressure to build, you'll have liquid to make your gravy that's well-seasoned and tasty, too.

Times will vary slightly depending on the kind of meat you are cooking but the size of the "chunk" is the biggest factor. Cubes of stewing beef will cook faster than a single roast.

To be sure you can always insert a meat thermometer to check for doneness.

Beef
Rare [52°C, 125°F] • Medium [63°C, 145°F] • Well [71°C, 160°F]

Lamb
Medium [63°C, 145°F] • Well [71°C, 160°F]

Pork
No less than [85°C, 185°F]

Chicken & Turkey
No less than [75°C, 165°F]

Ingredients

3 - 4 lbs (2 to 2.5 Kg) roast (I urge you to pay the extra for animals raised in ethical conditions. Also grass fed beef is worth every penny for the wonderful taste)
Herbs to taste, such as thyme, rosemary, basil, etc. (I often use Herbes de Provence)
12 ounces (350 mL) vegetable broth (or chicken or beef)

2 cloves of garlic, halved

3 - 4 large carrots, peeled and chunked

2 medium onions, quartered

1 or 2 bouillon cubes, packets or liquid

METHOD

1. Rub the roast well with the herbs of your choice and let it sit for an hour or so.

2. Pour the broth into the Instant Pot, add the garlic, place the trivet in the bottom and place the roast on the trivet.

3. Close and lock the lid ensuring the Pressure Valve is in the sealing position.

4. Select Meat/Stew mode and set the cooking time for 35 minutes.

5. When cooking time is up, use Natural Pressure Release for 10 minutes, then release the pressure.

6. Use a meat thermometer to check the internal temperature at the thickest part - but not touching a bone.

7. If the roast is done remove it and place on a warm platter and cover with aluminum foil.

8. Add the carrots and onions to the Instant Pot, close the lid, select the Manual/Pressure Cook setting for 5 minutes.

9. When cooking time is up, use Natural Pressure Release for 10 minutes and then release pressure.

10. Remove the carrots and onions to a warm serving dish and place in a 170°F, (77°C) oven to keep warm.

11. Remove the roast and allow it to sit for 5-10 minutes before carving.

12. Add an appropriate bouillon flavor cube, packet or liquid to the broth for the type of meat you are cooking.

13. Place a tablespoonful of cornstarch into a small cup and stir in just enough water to make it pourable.

14. Click the Sauté button on the Instant Pot to bring the broth to a simmer and slowly stir in the liquid cornstarch.

15. Stop adding the cornstarch when the gravy is the consistency of honey.

COTTAGE PIE

Traditional meets modern with the reinvention of this classic recipe for the Instant Pot.

Two trivets are required for this recipe - one with longer legs and the one that comes with your Instant Pot.

INGREDIENTS

For the ground beef (mince) part:
> 2 teaspoons (10 mL) olive oil
> 1 small onion, diced
> 1 medium carrot, peeled and diced
> 1 stalk of celery, diced
> 1½ cups (115g) white (button) mushrooms, sliced
> 2 cloves garlic, minced
> 1 teaspoon (5 mL) dried thyme
> 2 teaspoons (10 mL) Worcestershire sauce
> 2 tablespoons (30 mL) tomato paste
> 1 pound (454g) lean ground beef (mince)
> 1 cup (240 mL) beef broth, preferably homemade (see page 17 - Stock)
> 1 beef bouillon cube, crumbled or 1½ teaspoons (7.5 mL) liquid bouillon such as Bovril

Added later
> 1 cup (150g) frozen green peas

For the mashed potato part:
> 2 pounds (900g) potatoes, peeled and cut into 1½ inch (4 cm) cubes

Final additions
> ½ cup (120 mL) milk
> sea salt and freshly ground black pepper, to taste
> 1 teaspoon (5 mL) Worcestershire sauce

METHOD

1. Select Sauté mode and allow the inner pot to heat up.

2. Add the olive oil and allow it to heat up.

3. Add the onion, carrot, and celery and sauté 2-3 minutes.

4. Add the mushrooms and sauté for another minute.

5. Add the garlic, thyme, Worcestershire sauce, tomato paste and ground beef (mince).

6. Sauté until the ground beef (mince) is no longer pink.

7. Add the beef broth and use a wooden or silicone spatula to scrape any bits from the bottom of the pot.

8. Crumble the bouillon cube on top or add the liquid bouillon. Stir.

9. Press Cancel to turn off Sauté mode.

10. Place the tall trivet over the ground beef (mince) mixture and then place the regular trivet on top.

11. Place the potatoes on the trivet and fold the arms over top to allow easy removal.

12. Close and lock the lid ensuring the Pressure Valve is in the Sealing position.

13. Select Manual/Pressure Cook mode and set the cooking time for 12 minutes. (Push the "+" or "-" buttons to set the required cooking time.)

14. When cooking time is complete, use a Quick Release by carefully turning the Pressure Valve from Sealing to Venting.

15. Once all of the pressure has been released and the Float Valve has dropped, carefully remove the lid.

16. Place the potatoes in a separate bowl and mash, adding the milk and salt and pepper to taste.

17. Place the ground beef (mince) mixture is an oven-safe casserole dish, add the peas and stir. Add salt and pepper to taste.

18. Top the beef (mince) mixture with the mashed potatoes and drizzle with a little Worcestershire sauce.

19. Place under a broiler for 10-15 minutes or until the potato topping is golden brown.

Bangers & Mash

Quintessential pub grub in your Instant Pot? Yes!

Ingredients

For the potatoes

4 large potatoes, peeled and cut into 1½ inch (4 cm) cubes

1 cup (240 mL) water

For the mash step

½ cup (120 mL) milk

1 tablespoon (15 mL) butter

1 teaspoon (5 mL) dry mustard powder or 2 teaspoons (10 mL) Dijon or wholegrain mustard

Salt and pepper to taste

½ cup (50g) sharp (mature) Cheddar cheese, grated (optional)

For the sausages

4 large pork sausages, each lightly pierced with a sharp knife just once

2 teaspoons (10 mL) olive oil

½ cup (75 grams) onions, chopped

⅓ cup (80 mL) chutney of your choice

½ cup (120 mL) dry red wine

½ cup (120 mL) water

Thickener

1 tablespoon (15 mL) cornstarch

1 tablespoon (15 mL) cold water

Final addition

Salt and black pepper to taste

Method

Preparing the Potatoes

1. Preheat the oven (yes, your oven - we're just going to keep the potatoes warm while the sausages cook) to 225°F (110°C, Gas Mark ¼).

2. Place 1 cup (240 mL) water and a trivet in the inner pot of your Instant Pot.

3. Place the potato cubes in a steamer basket and place the steamer basket on the trivet.

4. Close and lock the lid ensuring that the Pressure Valve is in the Sealing position.

5. Select the Steam function and set the cooking time for 4 minutes. (Push the "+" or "-" buttons to set the required cooking time.)

6. Once the cooking time is complete do a Quick Release by carefully turning the Pressure Valve from Sealing to Venting.

7. Once all of the pressure has been released and the Float Valve has dropped, carefully remove the lid.

8. Remove the steam basket with the potatoes. Place the potatoes in an oven-safe dish and place in the oven to keep warm.

Preparing the Sausages

1. Discard the steaming water from the inner pot, dry the pot and return it to the Instant Pot.

2. Select Sauté function and adjust to "More" for higher heat.

   Tip: on some models you'll press the Adjust button once (after pressing Sauté) and on some models you'll press the Sauté button a second time to achieve "More".

3. Add the olive oil and allow it to heat up.

4. Add the sausages and brown. On "More" this should only take a couple of minutes. Just make sure all sides are slightly browned.

5. Add the onions, chutney, wine and water.

6. Press Cancel to turn off the Sauté function.

7. Close and lock the lid ensuring the Pressure Valve is in the Sealing position.

8. Select Meat/Stew function and set the cooking time for 8 minutes. (Push the "+" or "-" buttons to set the required cooking time.)

Back to the Potatoes While the Sausages Cook

1. Heat the milk for the mashed potatoes (you can do this in a microwave - but be careful because it can boil over very quickly).

2. Once the milk is hot stir in the butter, the mustard and some salt and pepper.

3. Mash the potatoes and mix in the milk mixture until the desired texture is reached.

4. Stir in the cheese (if using), cover with foil tightly and place in the oven to keep warm.

Back to the Sausages

1. Once the cooking time is complete do a Quick Release by carefully turning the Pressure Valve from Sealing to Venting.

2. Once all of the pressure has been released and the Float Valve has dropped, carefully remove the lid.

3. Select the Sauté function and thicken the sauce with the cornstarch mixture, stirring constantly until the desire consistency is achieved. Add salt and pepper to taste.

4. Press Cancel to turn off Sauté.

Putting it all Together

1. Equally divide the mashed potatoes between the plates and top with the sausages (bangers) and sauce.

2. Serve immediately.

Shepherd's Pie

Traditionally made with lamb - why do you think it's called shepherd's pie - but you can use beef.

Ingredients

For the Potato Topping

 2 pounds (1 Kg) potatoes, peeled and cut into large chunks

 ½ cup (120 mL) whole milk

 2 tablespoons (30g) butter

 ½ teaspoon (2.5 mL) sea salt

 ¼ teaspoon (1.25 mL) black pepper, freshly ground

 2 cups (200g) sharp (mature) Cheddar cheese, grated (optional)

For the Filling

 2 pounds (2 Kg) lean ground lamb, or lean ground beef (mince)

 1 cup (150g) onion, diced

 1 cup (150g) carrots, diced

 3 cloves garlic, chopped

 1 cup (120 mL) beef broth, preferably homemade (see page 17 - Stock)

 1 tablespoon (15 mL) tomato paste

 ½ teaspoon (2.5 mL) sea salt

 ½ teaspoon (2.5 mL) black pepper, freshly ground

 ½ cup (90g) frozen corn

 ½ cup (75g) frozen peas

 2 tablespoons (30 mL) cornstarch

 2 tablespoons (30 mL) water

 2 tablespoons (30 mL) fresh parsley, finely chopped (optional)

Method

Preheat the oven to 225°F (110°C, Gas Mark ¼). We'll be using the oven to keep the potatoes warm while the filling cooks.

We'll also use the oven, on broil, to brown the potato topping once the Shepherd's Pie has been put together.

For the Potato Topping

1. Add 1 cup (240 mL) water to the inner liner of your Instant Pot and place the trivet in the bottom.

2. Place the potatoes in a steamer basket and place the basket on top of the trivet.

3. Close and lock the lid ensuring the Pressure Valve is in the Sealing position.

4. Select the Steam function and set the cooking time for 5 minutes. (Push the "+" or "-" buttons to set the required cooking time.)

5. When cooking time is complete, do a Quick Release by carefully turning the Pressure Valve from Venting to Sealing.

6. Once all of the pressure has been released and the Float Valve has dropped, carefully remove the lid.

7. Remove the steamer basket from the Instant Pot and transfer the potatoes to a warm bowl.

8. Mash the potatoes and beat in the rest of the topping ingredients.

9. Cover the bowl with foil and place in the warm oven while you cook the filling ingredients.

For the Filling

1. Drain the water from the Instant Pot liner, wipe it dry and return it to the base.

2. Select Sauté mode and allow the inner liner to heat up.

3. Add the ground lamb (or beef) and sauté until no longer pink.

4. Remove the ground meat with a slotted spoon and then pour off any excess fat leaving behind about a tablespoon.

5. To the fat remaining in the pot, add the onions, carrots and garlic and sauté for 2-3 minutes.

6. Add the beef broth and use a wooden or silicone spatula to scrape any bits off the bottom of the pot.

7. Return the meat to the pot and add the tomato paste, salt and pepper. Mix well.

8. Close and lock the lid ensuring the Pressure Valve is in the Sealing Position.

9. Select Manual/Pressure Cook mode and set the cooking time for 3 minutes. (Push the "+" or "-" buttons to set the required cooking time.)

10. When cooking time is complete, do a Quick Release by carefully turning the Pressure Valve from Sealing to Venting.

11. Once all of the pressure has been released and the Float Valve has dropped, carefully remove the lid.

12. Select Sauté mode and bring the filling mixture to a light simmer.

13. Add the frozen peas and corn and stir well.

14. In a small dish or measuring cup, combine the cornstarch and water and mix to make a pourable paste.

15. Slowly drizzle the cornstarch mixture into the filling mixture, stirring constantly until the desired consistency is reach.

16. Add the parsley (if using) and stir well.

17. Press Cancel to turn off Sauté mode.

18. Carefully transfer the filling to an oven-safe, greased 9-inch (23 cm) deep pie plate.

19. Remove the Potato Topping mixture from the oven and turn the oven to broil.

20. Spread the Potato Topping over the filling and spread the topping to the edges of the pie plate.

21. Place the Shepherd's Pie under the broiler for about 5-10 minutes or until the topping is golden brown.

22. Remove from the oven, turn off the broiler and allow the pie to cool for about 5 minutes before serving.

A Side of Red Cabbage and Apple

This is a tasty side dish, particularly with pork. It can also be a vegetarian main or side dish. While the caraway seeds are optional, personally, I like the flavor it adds to this dish.

Ingredients

3 tablespoons (45 mL) red wine vinegar or balsamic vinegar
½ cup (120 mL) vegetable broth or water
1 pound (450g) red cabbage, quartered, cored and thinly sliced
1 teaspoon (5 mL) sea salt
½ teaspoon (2.5 mL) caraway seeds
½ teaspoon (2.5 mL) black pepper, freshly ground
¼ teaspoon (2.5 mL) nutmeg, freshly grated
¼ teaspoon (2.5 mL) ground cinnamon
¼ teaspoon (2.5 mL) ground cloves
3 tablespoons (30g) brown sugar
1 medium yellow onion, halved and thinly sliced
2 apples, halved, cored and thinly sliced
2 cloves garlic, minced

Method

1. Add the vegetable broth (or water) and vinegar to the inner liner of your Instant Pot.

   Tip: This recipe doesn't require the use of the Sauté function, so it's a good idea to take the inner liner out of your Instant Pot to the counter where you'll be working. You can then add and layer all the ingredients and place the inner liner back in the Instant Pot before cooking. This lessens the danger of getting any of the ingredients into the lid channel.

2. Create a layer of cabbage (about ¼ of the head), sprinkle with about ¼ of the caraway seeds, spices and brown sugar. Then layer about ¼ of the thinly sliced onions, apples and garlic. Repeat until all of the ingredients are used up.

3. Return the inner liner to the Instant Pot.

4. Close and lock the lid ensuring the Pressure Valve is in the Sealing position.

5. Select the Steam function and set the cooking time for 3 minutes. (Push the "+" or "-" buttons to set the required cooking time.)

6. Once the cooking time is complete, do a Quick Release by carefully turning the Pressure Valve from Sealing to Venting.

7. Once all of the pressure is released and the Float Valve has dropped, carefully remove the lid.

8. Stir well and serve immediately.

Cider Pot Roast Shoulder Of Lamb

The hard cider in this recipe not only adds a bit of a tang, it also works like a tenderizer, too. Be sure to use all of the leftover liquid to make an amazing gravy for this tasty one-pot meal.

Ingredients

1 tablespoon (15 mL) butter
3½ pound (1½ Kg) lean, boneless shoulder of lamb, rolled and tied
2 medium onions, halved and sliced
2 cups (500 mL) hard cider (like Strongbow)
1 cup (240 mL) lamb broth, or chicken broth or vegetable broth, preferably homemade
(see page 17 - Stock)
1½ pounds (680g) small potatoes, scrubbed
1½ pounds (680g) baby carrots
4 small turnips, peeled and cut in half (these are the white turnips with purple tops)
1 small orange, juiced
peel from half of the orange, cut into thin strips
1 tablespoon (15 mL) fresh thyme leaves or 1 teaspoon (5 mL) dried thyme
1 teaspoon (5 mL) sea salt
½ teaspoon (2.5 mL) black pepper, freshly ground
¾ cup (180 mL) liquid honey

Method

1. Select Sauté mode and allow the inner liner of your Instant Pot to heat up.
2. Add the butter and let it heat up and get bubbly.
3. Add the lamb roast and gently seared it on all sides. Then remove the roast and set aside.
4. Add the onions and sauté for 2-3 minutes.
5. Press Cancel to turn off Sauté mode.

6. Add the cider and the broth. Use a wooden or silicone spatula to scrape any bits off the bottom of the pot.

7. Add the rest of the ingredients, except for the honey, and stir well. (Note: We'll add the honey later, when the roast is done.)

8. Place the roast on top.

9. Close and lock the lid ensuring the Pressure Valve is in the Sealing position.

10. Select the Meat/Stew mode and set the cooking time for 50 minutes. (Push the "+" or "-" buttons to set the required cooking time.)

11. Once cooking time is complete do a Quick Release by carefully turning the Pressure Valve from Sealing to Venting.

12. When all of the pressure has been released and the Float Valve has dropped, carefully remove the lid.

13. Remove the roast to a warm serving platter.

14. With a slotted spoon, remove the vegetables to a warm bowl.

15. Select Sauté mode and bring the remaining liquid to a light simmer.

16. Add the honey and mix well to ensure it is fully dissolved in the liquid.

17. To thicken the liquid, combine approximately 1 tablespoon (15 mL) of cornstarch and 1 tablespoon (15 mL) of water, and stir to make a pourable paste.

18. Slowly drizzle the cornstarch mixture into the simmering liquid, stirring constantly until the desired consistency is reached.

19. Press Cancel to turn off Sauté mode.

20. Slice the lamb and serve with the vegetables and gravy.

Marinated Pork Loin Roast

Start this recipe the day before as the pork roast needs to be marinated for up to 24 hours.

Ingredients For Marinade

3-4 pound (1½ - 2 Kg) boneless pork loin roast
6-8 garlic cloves, sliced into thin slivers
¼ cup (60 mL) extra virgin olive oil
1 fresh lemon, juiced
1 teaspoon (5 mL) fennel seed
1 teaspoon (5 mL) dried oregano leaves

Ingredients To Roast

6-8 slices bacon (streaky bacon), chopped
2-3 medium yellow onions, quartered
2 stalks celery, chunked
2½ cups (600 mL) full-bodied dry red wine
1 cup (120 mL) chicken or vegetable broth, preferably homemade (see page 17 - Stock)

Method

Marinating the Roast

1. Using a small, very sharp knife, create several fairly deep slits all over the pork roast. Insert a sliver of garlic into each slit.

2. Place the roast in a sealable plastic bag that is large enough to hold the roast and the marinade.

3. In a small glass bowl combine the olive oil, lemon juice, fennel seeds and oregano. Mix well.

4. Pour the marinade over the roast, remove most of the air from the bag and seal.

5. Place the roast in the refrigerator for up to 24 hours (6 hours minimum). Turn the roast every few hours, or

whenever you think about it, to make sure the roast gets well marinated.

Cooking the Roast

1. Select Sauté mode and allow the inner liner of your Instant Pot to heat up.

2. Put the chopped bacon in the pot and sauté for 4-5 minutes.

3. Add the onions and celery and sauté for another 2-3 minutes.

4. Add the red wine and use a wooden or silicone spatula to scrape any bits from the bottom of the pot.

5. Press Cancel to turn off Sauté.

6. Add the broth and stir well.

7. Place the trivet in the pot and place the marinated pork roast on the trivet.

8. Close and lock the lid ensuring the Pressure Valve is in the Sealing position.

9. Select the Meat/Stew function and set the cooking time for 45 minutes. (Push the "+" or "-" buttons to set the required cooking time.)

10. When cooking time is complete allow a Natural Pressure Release for 10-15 minutes and then release the rest of the pressure by carefully turning the Pressure Valve from Sealing to Venting.

11. Once all of the pressure has been released, and the Float Valve has dropped, carefully remove the lid.

12. Remove the roast to a warm plate and cover.

13. To make a gravy from the liquid, press the Sauté and bring the liquid to a light simmer.

14. While that is happening, mix together approximately 1 tablespoon (15 mL) of cornstarch and 1 tablespoon (15 mL) of water to make a pourable paste.

15. Slowly drizzle the cornstarch mixture into the liquid, stirring constantly, until the desired consistency is reached.

16. Press Cancel to turn off Sauté mode.
17. Slice and serve the pork roast with the gravy and potatoes and vegetables of your choice.

APPLESAUCE

Applesauce is a great addition to any pork roast Sunday dinner. This is an easy recipe to make yourself using the Instant Pot.

You'll find lots of applesauce recipes that tell you to peel the apples, I don't. Why? There are lots of nutrients in apple skin and flavor, too!

Some recipes will also suggest sweetening the applesauce, I don't. Why? Apples are naturally sweet, there's no need to add additional sweeteners.

INGREDIENTS

6 - 8 medium to large apples (Granny Smith, Gala, McIntosh, Fuji, etc.), well washed
1 cup (240 mL) water
1 teaspoon (5 mL) lemon juice (freshly squeezed, if possible)

METHOD

1. Cut the well-washed apples into halves and then quarters. Remove the core and seeds then cut the quarters into 2" (5 cm) chunks.

2. Place the apples in the Instant Pot along with 1 cup (240 mL) of water and 1 teaspoon (5 mL) lemon juice.

3. Close and lock the lid ensuring the Pressure Valve is in the Sealing position.

4. Select Manual/Pressure Cook mode and set the cooking time for 8 minutes.

5. Once the cooking time is complete, allow a Natural Pressure Release for 1 - 3 minutes and then release the rest of the pressure by carefully turning the Pressure Valve from Sealing to Venting.

   Tip: If you experience some applesauce spewing out of the Pressure Valve, turn it back to Sealing, wait a few more minutes and try again.

6. When all of the pressure has been released, and the Float Valve has dropped, carefully open and remove the lid. Use an electric

mixer or immersion blender to attain applesauce consistency. Alternately, you can place the cooked apples in a food processor.

7. Allow the applesauce to cool somewhat and then put it in clean, sterilized (running them through the dishwasher should be enough) mason jars and refrigerate.

Note: Homemade applesauce will be okay in the fridge for about a week. It also freezes well and you can keep it in the freezer for up to a year.

HOTPOTS

Traditionally a "Lancashire Hotpot" was a stew with meat (originally mutton), onions and potatoes that was cooked all day, in a heavy iron pot over an open fire.

The farmer's wife could keep an eye on it and the long cooking time would tenderize the potentially tough meat.

Essentially they are a casserole, somewhere between a soup and a stew. The meat and vegetables are topped with a layer of thinly sliced potatoes.

INSTANT POT HOT POTS

Yes, you can certainly do this traditional British dish in your Instant Pot. We're going to do it in two steps but, not to worry, it's easy. Actually, three steps if you include finishing it off in the broiler to get those nice crispy potatoes on top.

In our Instant Pot versions we are cooking the meat and vegetables separately from the potato slices then combining the two in individual onion soup bowls which go under the grill to turn golden brown.

ORIGINAL LANCASHIRE HOTPOT
(FROM WIKIPEDIA)
Included for historical interest

Originating from England, is a very easy but delicious dish that consists of lamb, onions, potatoes and the cook's choice of herbs. This is baked in an oven.

INGREDIENTS

2 lb (900g) neck of lamb or mutton
2 large potatoes
1 large or 2 small white onion(s)
Choice of mixed herbs
500 mL boiling water

METHOD

1. Dice the lamb and set aside. Preheat oven to 325F / 170C / Gas Mark 3.

2. Slice the potatoes and dice the onions.

3. Add a layer of the potatoes to the bottom of a casserole dish, and cover with a handful of the diced onion. Layer the diced lamb on top of this, sprinkling with your choice of herbs.

4. Repeat these layers until the dish is full. Top with a final layer of the potatoes.

5. Pour boiling water into the dish until filled - if more water is needed, continue to add until topped.

6. Bake for at least one hour, though traditionally the dish was left baking all day, longer times are required for Mutton.

A handful of mixed vegetables such as parsnips, turnips, leek or carrots can be added to the dish. It is worth experimenting to find out what combination of flavours you prefer.

The dish has occasionally been known to be cooked with oysters or with small birds such as snipe, when they were available.

Traditional Lancashire Hot Pot

Ingredients For Potato Layer

2 pounds (900g) potatoes, thinly sliced (you can peel them if you like, I prefer to leave the skins on)
1 cup (240 mL) water
ice bath

Ingredients For Filling

2 pounds (900g) lamb, cut into bite-size pieces
¼ cup (30g) all-purpose flour
1 teaspoon (5 mL) sea salt
½ teaspoon (2.5 mL) black pepper, freshly ground
3 lamb kidneys, well rinsed, fat removed and sliced (optional)
¼ cup (60g) butter, divided
2 medium onions, chopped
4 large carrots, chopped
3 cups (700 mL) chicken or vegetable broth, preferably homemade (see page 17 - Stock)
2 teaspoons (10 mL) Worcestershire sauce
2 bay leaves

Ingredients For Topping

2 tablespoons (30g) butter, melted

Method

Preparing the Potatoes

1. Arrange the thinly sliced potatoes in a steaming basket.

2. Place 1 cup (240 mL) of water and a trivet in the inner liner of your Instant Pot.

3. Place the steaming basket with the sliced potatoes on the trivet.

4. Close and lock the lid, ensuring that the Pressure Valve is in the Sealing position.

5. Select the Steam function and set the cooking time for 1 minute.

6. Once the cooking time is complete, do a Quick Release by carefully turning the Pressure Valve to Venting.

7. Once all of the pressure has been released and the Float Valve has dropped, carefully open and remove the lid.

8. Carefully remove the steaming basket and plunge the potatoes into an ice bath to stop the cooking process.

9. Once the potatoes have cooled, drain the water and place the potato slices on several layers of paper towel. Dab them with more paper towel. You want them to be as dry as possible. Cover and set aside.

Preparing the Hot Pot Filling

1. Place the lamb and kidney (if using) in a medium bowl and sprinkle with the salt, pepper and flour. Toss to make sure everything is well coated.

2. Select Sauté mode on your Instant Pot and allow the inner liner to heat up.

3. Add 2 tablespoons (30g) of butter and allow it to heat up and get bubbly.

4. In batches, brown the lamb and kidney (if using), and set aside.

5. Add the other 2 tablespoons (30g) of butter to the inner liner and allow it to melt and get bubbly.

6. Add the onions and carrots and sauté for 3-4 minutes.

7. Add 2-3 tablespoons (30-45 mL) of the broth and use a wooden or silicone spatula to scrape any bits off the bottom of the pot.

8. Press the Cancel button to turn off Sauté mode.

9. Add the rest of the broth, the Worcestershire sauce, the bay leaves and the browned lamb and kidney (if using).

10. Close and lock the lid, ensuring that the Pressure Valve is in the Sealing position.

11. Select Meat/Stew mode and set the cooking time for 35 minutes. (Tip: If you have not changed the factory presets, when you select the Meat/Stew function it should automatically default to a 35 minute cooking time. Otherwise, just push the "+" or "-" buttons to set the required cooking time.)

12. When the cooking time is complete, allow a Natural Pressure Release for at least 15 minutes.

13. Turn the Pressure Valve to Venting to release any remaining pressure and, when the Float Valve has dropped, carefully open and remove the lid.

14. If the filling requires thickening, create a thin paste by combining, in a small bowl, approximately 1 tablespoon (15 mL) of cornstarch and enough water to create a pourable paste.

15. Select the Sauté button and allow the filling to come to simmer.

16. Stir in the cornstarch mixture, a little at a time, until the desired thickness has been achieved. Then press Cancel to turn off Sauté mode.

17. Remove the bay leaves.

Putting the Hot Pot Together

1. Ladle the filling equally between 6 broiler-safe French Onion soup bowls (or something similar - just make sure the dish is broiler-safe).

2. Arrange the pre-cooked potato slices on top in a concentric circle.

3. Brush the top of the potatoes with the melted butter and broil for 5-10 minutes, until the potatoes are brown and crispy.

4. Carefully remove the Hot Pots from the broiler and serve immediately.

   Tip: You may want to arrange the Hot Pots on a cookie sheet before putting them in the broiler. This makes it a little easier to get them in and out of the oven. Also, some of the dishes may bubble over, so it also contains any drips.

Tip: You can also make one large Hot Pot in a casserole dish, if you prefer. Just make sure the casserole dish is broiler safe.

Hearty Vegetarian Hot Pot

For those who prefer to eat vegetarian, either all the time or occasionally, this recipe will satisfy your craving for a hearty Hot Pot.

Ingredients For Potato Layer

2 pounds (900g) potatoes, thinly sliced (you can peel them if you like, I prefer to leave the skins on)
1 cup (240 mL) water
ice bath

Ingredients For Filling

2 tablespoons (30 mL) olive oil
1 medium yellow onion, sliced
1 clove garlic, minced
5 stalks celery, thick sliced
1 tablespoon (15 mL) fresh thyme, chopped or 1 teaspoon (5 mL) dried thyme
1 cup (240 mL) dry sherry or dry white wine
1 vegetable bouillon cube, crumbled
2 tablespoons (30 mL) tomato paste
1 teaspoon (5 mL) low sodium soy sauce
2 cups (480 mL) vegetable broth, preferably homemade (see page 17 - Stock)
¼ cup (55g) basmati rice (or white rice of your choice)
1 tablespoon (15 mL) fresh thyme, chopped or 1 teaspoon (5 mL) dried thyme
1 teaspoon (5 mL) sea salt
½ teaspoon (2.5 mL) black pepper, freshly ground
3 large parsnips, peeled and cut into bite-size chunks
3 large carrots, peeled and cut into bite-size chunks

Ingredients For Topping

2 tablespoons (30g) butter, melted (use vegan butter if you want this recipe to be vegan)

METHOD

Preparing the Potatoes

1. Arrange the thinly sliced potatoes in a steaming basket.

2. Place 1 cup (240 mL) of water and a trivet in the inner liner of your Instant Pot.

3. Place the steaming basket with the sliced potatoes on the trivet.

4. Close and lock the lid, ensuring that the Pressure Valve is in the Sealing position.

5. Select the Steam function and set the cooking time for 1 minute.

6. Once the cooking time is complete, do a Quick Release by carefully turning the Pressure Valve to Venting.

7. Once all of the pressure has been released and the Float Valve has dropped, carefully open and remove the lid.

8. Carefully remove the steaming basket and plunge the potatoes into an ice bath to stop the cooking process.

9. Once the potatoes have cooled, drain the water and place the potato slices on several layers of paper towel. Dab them with more paper towel. You want them to be as dry as possible. Cover them and set them aside.

Preparing the Hot Pot Filling

1. Select Sauté mode on your Instant Pot and allow the inner liner to heat up.

2. Add the olive oil and allow it to heat up.

3. Add the onions, garlic and celery and sauté for 3-4 minutes.

4. Add the thyme and stir well.

5. Slowly pour in the sherry (or white wine), while using a wooden or silicone spatula to scrape up any bits on the bottom of the pot.

6. Press the Cancel button to turn off Sauté mode.

7. Add the rest of the ingredients (with the exception of the potatoes you have set aside) and stir well.

8. Close and lock the lid, ensuring that the Pressure Valve is in the Sealing position.

9. Select Manual/Pressure Cook mode and set the cooking time for 5 minutes. (Push the "+" or "-" buttons to set the required cooking time.)

10. When the cooking time is complete, allow a Natural Pressure Release for at least 5 minutes.

11. Turn the Pressure Valve to Venting to release any remaining pressure and, when the Float Valve has dropped, carefully open and remove the lid.

12. If the filling requires thickening, create a thin paste by combining, in a small bowl, approximately 1 tablespoon (15 mL) of cornstarch and enough water to create a pourable paste.

13. Select the Sauté button and allow the filling to come to a simmer.

14. Stir in the cornstarch mixture, a little at a time, until the desired thickness has been achieved.

Putting the Hot Pot Together

1. Ladle the filling equally between 6 broiler-safe French Onion soup bowls (or something similar - just make sure the dish is boiler-safe).

2. Arrange the pre-cooked potato slices on top in a concentric circle.

3. Brush the top of the potatoes with the melted butter and broil for 5-10 minutes, until the potatoes are brown and crispy.

4. Carefully remove the Hot Pots from the broiler and serve immediately.

   Tip: You may want to arrange the Hot Pots on a cookie sheet before putting them in the broiler. This makes it a little easier to get them in and out of the oven. Also, some of the dishes may bubble over, so it also contains any drips.

Beef Hotpot

Ingredients For Potato Layer

2 pounds (900g) potatoes, thinly sliced (you can peel them if you like, I prefer to leave the skins on)
1 cup (240 mL) water
ice bath

Ingredients For Filling

2 pounds (900g) Chuck steak or roast, cut into bite-size pieces
1 teaspoon (5 mL) sea salt
½ teaspoon (2.5 mL) black pepper, freshly ground
2 tablespoons (15g) all purpose flour
2 tablespoons (30g) butter
1 tablespoon (15 mL) olive oil
1 large yellow onion, halved and sliced
1 stalk celery, sliced
3 cloves garlic, minced
1 teaspoon (5 mL) dried marjoram or 1 tablespoon (15 mL) fresh marjoram, minced
1 cup (240 mL) dry red wine
2 cups (480 mL) beef broth, preferably homemade (see page 17 - Stock)
1 beef bouillon cube, crumbled
4 large carrots, peeled and cut into bite-size pieces
1 bay leaf

Ingredients For Topping

2 tablespoons (30g) melted butter

Method

Preparing the Potatoes

1. Arrange the thinly sliced potatoes in a steaming basket.

2. Place 1 cup (240 mL) of water and a trivet in the inner liner of your Instant Pot.

3. Place the steaming basket with the sliced potatoes on the trivet.

4. Close and lock the lid, ensuring that the Pressure Valve is in the Sealing position.

5. Select the Steam function and set the cooking time for 1 minute.

6. Once the cooking time is complete, do a Quick Release by carefully turning the Pressure Valve to Venting.

7. Once all of the pressure has been released and the Float Valve has dropped, carefully open and remove the lid.

8. Carefully remove the steaming basket and plunge the potatoes into an ice bath to stop the cooking process.

9. Once the potatoes have cooled, drain the water and place the potato slices on several layers of paper towel. Dab them with more paper towel. You want them to be as dry as possible. Cover them and set them aside.

Preparing the Hot Pot Filling

1. Place the cut up beef in a medium bowl and sprinkle with the salt, pepper and flour. Toss to make sure everything is well coated.

2. Select Sauté mode on your Instant Pot and allow the inner liner to heat up.

3. Add 2 tablespoons (30g) of butter and allow it to heat up and get bubbly.

4. In batches, brown the beef, and set aside.

5. Add the tablespoon (15g) of olive oil to the inner liner and allow it to heat up.

6. Add the onion, celery and garlic and sauté for 3-4 minutes.

7. Add the marjoram and mix well.

8. Add 2-3 tablespoons (30-45 mL) of the red wine and use a wooden or silicone spatula to scrape any bits off the bottom of the pot.

9. Press the Cancel button to turn off Sauté mode.

10. Add the rest of the red wine, as well as the broth, crumbled bouillon cube, carrots, bay leaf and the browned beef cubes.

11. Close and lock the lid, ensuring that the Pressure Valve is in the Sealing position.

12. Select Meat/Stew mode and set the cooking time for 20 minutes.

    Tip: If you have not changed the factory presets, when you select the Meat/Stew function it should automatically default to a 35 minute cooking time. Press the Adjust button twice to display 20 minutes. If your Instant Pot doesn't have an Adjust button, press the Meat/Stew button until it displays 20 minutes. Otherwise, just push the "+" or "-" buttons to set the required cooking time.

13. When the cooking time is complete, allow a Natural Pressure Release for at least 15 minutes.

14. Turn the Pressure Valve to Venting to release any remaining pressure and, when the Float Valve has dropped, carefully open and remove the lid.

15. If the filling requires thickening, create a thin paste by combining, in a small bowl, approximately 1 tablespoon (15 mL) of cornstarch and enough water to create a pourable paste.

16. Select the Sauté button and allow the filling to come to a simmer.

17. Stir in the cornstarch mixture, a little at a time, until the desired thickness has been achieved. Then press Cancel to turn off Sauté mode.

18. Remove the bay leaf.

Putting the Hot Pot Together

1. Ladle the filling equally between 6 broiler-safe French Onion soup bowls (or something similar - just make sure the dish is boiler-safe).

2. Arrange the pre-cooked potato slices on top in a concentric circle.

3. Brush the top of the potatoes with the melted butter and broil for 5-10 minutes, until the potatoes are brown and crispy.

4. Carefully remove the Hot Pots from the broiler and serve immediately.

Tip: You may want to arrange the Hot Pots on a cookie sheet before putting them in the broiler. This makes it a little easier to get them in and out of the oven. Also, some of the dishes may bubble over, so it also contains any drips.

Tip: You can also make one large Hot Pot in a casserole dish, if you prefer. Just make sure the casserole dish is broiler safe.

Chicken & Ginger Hotpot

This hot pot has a bit of an Asian twist to it with the addition of ginger, soy sauce and coriander.

INGREDIENTS FOR POTATO LAYER

2 pounds (900g) potatoes, thinly sliced (you can peel them if you like, I prefer to leave the skins on)
1 cup (240 mL) water
ice bath

INGREDIENTS FOR FILLING

2 pounds (900g) boneless skinless chicken thighs, cut into bite size pieces
¼ cup (30g) all-purpose flour
1 teaspoon (5 mL) sea salt
½ teaspoon (2.5 mL) black pepper, freshly ground
2 tablespoons (30 mL) olive oil
1 inch (2.5 cm) piece fresh ginger, peeled and chopped
3 cloves garlic, chopped
1 medium yellow onion, halved and sliced
3 cups (700 mL) chicken or vegetable broth, preferably homemade (see page 17 - Stock)
2 tablespoons (30 mL) soy sauce
1 tablespoon (15 mL) brown sugar
1 cup (150g) fresh green beans, cut into 1 inch (2.5 cm) pieces

INGREDIENTS FOR TOPPING

2 tablespoons (30g) butter, melted

METHOD

Preparing the Potatoes

1. Arrange the thinly sliced potatoes in a steaming basket.

2. Place 1 cup (240 mL) of water and a trivet in the inner liner of your Instant Pot.

3. Place the steaming basket with the sliced potatoes on the trivet.

4. Close and lock the lid, ensuring that the Pressure Valve is in the Sealing position.

5. Select the Steam function and set the cooking time for 1 minute.

6. Once the cooking time is complete, do a Quick Release by carefully turning the Pressure Valve to Venting.

7. Once all of the pressure has been released and the Float Valve has dropped, carefully open and remove the lid.

8. Carefully remove the steaming basket and plunge the potatoes into an ice bath to stop the cooking process.

9. Once the potatoes have cooled, drain the water and place the potato slices on several layers of paper towel. Dab them with more paper towel. You want them to be as dry as possible. Cover and set aside.

Preparing the Hot Pot Filling

1. Place the cut up chicken thighs in a medium bowl and sprinkle with the flour, salt and pepper. Toss to make sure everything is well coated.

2. Select Sauté mode on your Instant Pot and allow the inner liner to heat up.

3. Once the inner pot is hot, add 1 tablespoon (15 mL) of the olive and allow it to heat up.

4. Add the coated chicken thighs and sauté until the are no longer pink.

5. Remove the chicken thighs and set aside.

6. Add the other tablespoon (15 mL) of olive oil to the pot and allow it to heat up.

7. Add the ginger, onion and garlic and sauté for 2-3 minutes.

8. Press Cancel to turn off Sauté mode.

9. Add the chicken broth and use a wooden or silicone spatula to scrape any bits off the bottom of the pot.

10. Return the chicken to the pot, add the soy sauce, brown sugar and green beans and stir.

11. Close and lock the lid, ensuring that the Pressure Valve is in the Sealing position.

12. Select Manual/Pressure Cook mode and set the cooking time for 10 minutes. (Push the "+" or "-" buttons to set the required cooking time.)

13. When the cooking time is complete, allow a Natural Pressure Release for 10 minutes.

14. Turn the Pressure Valve to Venting to release any remaining pressure and, when the Float Valve has dropped, carefully open and remove the lid.

15. If the filling requires thickening, create a thin paste by combining, in a small bowl, approximately 1 tablespoon (15 mL) of cornstarch and enough water to create a pourable paste.

16. Select the Sauté button and allow the filling to come to simmer.

17. Stir in the cornstarch mixture, a little at a time, until the desired thickness has been achieved. Then press Cancel to turn off Sauté mode.

Putting the Hot Pot Together

1. Ladle the filling equally between 4 broiler-safe French Onion soup bowls (or something similar - just make sure the dish is boiler-safe).

2. Arrange the pre-cooked potato slices on top in a concentric circle.

3. Brush the top of the potatoes with the melted butter and broil for 5-10 minutes, until the potatoes are brown and crispy.

4. Carefully remove the Hot Pots from the broiler and serve immediately.

Tip: You may want to arrange the Hot Pots on a cookie sheet before putting them in the broiler. This makes it a little easier to get them in and out of the oven. Also, some of the dishes may bubble over, so it also contains any drips.

Tip: You can also make one large Hot Pot in a casserole dish, if you prefer. Just make sure the casserole dish is broiler safe.

Option: If you prefer, you can just make the Hot Pot filling and serve it over steamed rice.

Liver And Onion Hotpot

The taste of a liver and onion dinner, but in a Hot Pot.

Ingredients For Potato Layer

2 pounds (900g) potatoes, thinly sliced (you can peel them if you like, I prefer to leave the skins on)
1 cup (240 mL) water
ice bath

Ingredients For Filling

1 pound (454g) beef liver, cut into bite-size pieces (or liver of your choice)
2 tablespoons (15g) all purpose flour
1 teaspoon (5 mL) sea salt
½ teaspoon (2.5 mL) black pepper, freshly ground
3 to 4 slices of bacon (streaky bacon), chopped
2 medium yellow onions, halved and sliced
1 cup (150g) rutabaga (Swede), chopped
1 cup (150g) carrots, chopped
3 cups (700 mL) beef broth, preferably homemade
 (see page 17 - Stock)
1 tablespoon (15 mL) fresh sage, chopped or ½ teaspoon (2.5 mL) dried sage
1 tablespoon (15 mL) brown mustard seeds

Ingredients For Topping

2 tablespoons (30g) butter, melted

Method

Preparing the Potatoes

1. Arrange the thinly sliced potatoes in a steaming basket.

2. Place 1 cup (240 mL) of water and a trivet in the inner liner of your Instant Pot.

3. Place the steaming basket with the sliced potatoes on the trivet.

4. Close and lock the lid, ensuring that the Pressure Valve is in the Sealing position.

5. Select the Steam function and set the cooking time for 1 minute.

6. Once the cooking time is complete, do a Quick Release by carefully turning the Pressure Valve to Venting.

7. Once all of the pressure has been released and the Float Valve has dropped, carefully open and remove the lid.

8. Carefully remove the steaming basket and plunge the potatoes into an ice bath to stop the cooking process.

9. Once the potatoes have cooled, drain the water and place the potato slices on several layers of paper towel. Dab them with more paper towel. You want them to be as dry as possible. Cover and set aside.

Preparing the Hot Pot Filling

1. Place the cut up liver in a medium bowl and sprinkle with the flour, salt and pepper. Toss to make sure everything is well coated.

2. Select Sauté mode on your Instant Pot and allow the inner liner to heat up.

3. Once the inner pot is hot, add the bacon to the pot and sauté for 3-4 minutes.

4. Add the coated liver and sauté for an additional 2-3 minutes.

5. Remove the liver and bacon and set aside.

6. Add the onions and sauté for 2-3 minutes.

7. Press Cancel to turn off Sauté mode.

8. Add the broth and use a wooden or silicone spatula to scrape any bits off the bottom of the pot.

9. Return the liver and bacon to the pot and add the sage and mustard seed. Stir well.

10. Close and lock the lid, ensuring that the Pressure Valve is in the Sealing position.

11. Select Manual/Pressure Cook mode and set the cooking time for 10 minutes. (Push the "+" or "-" buttons to set the required cooking time.)

12. When the cooking time is complete, allow a Natural Pressure Release for 10 minutes.

13. Turn the Pressure Valve to Venting to release any remaining pressure and, when the Float Valve has dropped, carefully open and remove the lid.

14. If the filling requires thickening, create a thin paste by combining, in a small bowl, approximately 1 tablespoon (15 mL) of cornstarch and enough water to create a pourable paste.

15. Select the Sauté button and allow the filling to come to a simmer.

16. Stir in the cornstarch mixture, a little at a time, until the desired thickness has been achieved. Then press Cancel to turn off Sauté mode.

Putting the Hot Pot Together

1. Ladle the filling equally between 4 broiler-safe French Onion soup bowls (or something similar - just make sure the dish is broiler-safe).

2. Arrange the pre-cooked potato slices on top in a concentric circle.

3. Brush the top of the potatoes with the melted butter and broil for 5-10 minutes, until the potatoes are brown and crispy.

4. Carefully remove the Hot Pots from the broiler and serve immediately.

   Tip: You may want to arrange the Hot Pots on a cookie sheet before putting them in the broiler. This makes it a little easier to get them in and out of the oven. Also, some of the dishes may bubble over, so it also contains any drips.

   Tip: You can also make one large Hot Pot in a casserole dish, if you prefer. Just make sure the casserole dish is broiler safe.

Minced Beef (Hamburger) Hot Pot

A tasty Hot Pot with a hint of horseradish. Make this one on a cool evening and serve it with some fresh-from-the-oven crusty bread.

Interesting fact about rutabaga (Swede). According to Wikipedia it is a cross between a turnip and a cabbage. It was also referred to as a Swedish turnip, hence the name that most Europeans know it by - Swede. The name rutabaga actually comes from an old Swedish word.

Ingredients For Potato Layer

1 pound (454g) potatoes, thinly sliced (you can peel them if you like, I prefer to leave the skins on)
1 cup (240 mL) water
ice bath

Ingredients For Filling

1 pound (454g) lean ground beef
2 tablespoons (30 mL) olive oil
2 medium yellow onions, halved and sliced
2 cloves garlic, minced
1 stalk celery, sliced
1 teaspoon (5 mL) sea salt
½ teaspoon (2.5 mL) black pepper, freshly ground
1 tablespoon (15 mL) Worcestershire Sauce
1 tablespoon (15 mL) freshly grated horseradish or prepared horseradish
1½ cups (225g) rutabaga (Swede), peeled and diced
2 large carrots, peeled and cut into bite-size pieces
2 parsnips, peeled and cut into bite-size pieces
1 cup (150g) fresh or frozen peas
2 cups (475 mL) beef broth, preferably homemade (see page 17 - Stock)
1 beef bouillon cube, crumbled

INGREDIENTS FOR TOPPING

2 tablespoons (30g) butter, melted

METHOD

Preparing the Potatoes

1. Arrange the thinly sliced potatoes in a steaming basket.

2. Place 1 cup (240 mL) of water and a trivet in the inner liner of your Instant Pot.

3. Place the steaming basket with the sliced potatoes on the trivet.

4. Close and lock the lid, ensuring that the Pressure Valve is in the Sealing position.

5. Select the Steam function and set the cooking time for 1 minute.

6. Once the cooking time is complete, do a Quick Release by carefully turning the Pressure Valve to Venting.

7. Once all of the pressure has been released and the Float Valve has dropped, carefully open and remove the lid.

8. Carefully remove the steaming basket and plunge the potatoes into an ice bath to stop the cooking process.

9. Once the potatoes have cooled, drain the water and place the potato slices on several layers of paper towel. Dab them with more paper towel. You want them to be as dry as possible. Cover and set aside.

Preparing the Hot Pot Filling

1. Select Sauté mode on your Instant Pot and allow the inner liner to heat up.

2. Once the inner pot is hot, add the ground beef and sauté until it is no longer pink. Remove the ground beef and set aside, straining off any fat.

3. Add the olive oil to the pot and allow it to heat up.

4. Add the onions, garlic and celery and sauté for 2-3 minutes.

5. Press Cancel to turn off Sauté mode.

6. Return the ground beef to the pot and add a little of the broth. Use a wooden or silicone spatula to scrape any bits off the bottom of the pot.

7. Add the rest of the filling ingredients and stir well.

8. Close and lock the lid, ensuring that the Pressure Valve is in the Sealing position.

9. Select Manual/Pressure Cook mode and set the cooking time for 4 minutes. (Push the "+" or "-" buttons to set the required cooking time.)

10. When the cooking time is complete, allow a Natural Pressure Release for 5 minutes.

11. Turn the Pressure Valve to Venting to release any remaining pressure and, when the Float Valve has dropped, carefully open and remove the lid.

12. If the filling requires thickening, create a thin paste by combining, in a small bowl, approximately 1 tablespoon (15 mL) of cornstarch and enough water to create a pourable paste.

13. Select the Sauté button and allow the filling to come to a simmer.

14. Stir in the cornstarch mixture, a little at a time, until the desired thickness has been achieved. Then press Cancel to turn off Sauté mode.

Putting the Hot Pot Together

1. Ladle the filling equally between 4 broiler-safe French Onion soup bowls (or something similar - just make sure the dish is boiler-safe).

2. Arrange the pre-cooked potato slices on top in a concentric circle.

3. Brush the top of the potatoes with the melted butter and broil for 5-10 minutes, until the potatoes are brown and crispy.

4. Carefully remove the Hot Pots from the broiler and serve immediately.

Tip: You may want to arrange the Hot Pots on a cookie sheet before putting them in the broiler. This makes it a little easier to get them in and out of the oven. Also, some of the dishes may bubble over, so it also contains any drips.

Tip: You can also make one large Hot Pot in a casserole dish, if you prefer. Just make sure the casserole dish is broiler safe.

STEAK AND KIDNEY HOTPOT WITH CRUSTY DUMPLINGS

This is a little twist on an old favorite that combines two recipes in this book you may have already tried.

We'll be using the <u>Steak and Kidney Stew</u> recipes (see page 36) and one of the <u>dumpling recipes</u> (see page 58).

While the Steak and Kidney Stew is made in your Instant Pot, the Hot Pot, with the dumplings on top, will be baked in a hot oven so you can achieve the crusty dumplings.

INGREDIENTS FOR THE FILLING

<u>Steak and Kidney Stew</u> (see page 36) you can make it fresh or reheat as much as you need from the day before. It's usually better if the flavours have had a chance to mature.

INGREDIENTS FOR THE DUMPLINGS

Pick one of the <u>dumpling recipes</u> in this book (see page 58) - just be sure you make them fresh.

Feel free to add in spices of your choice. Here's some suggestions:

1-2 tablespoon (15-30 mL) freshly parsley, chopped
A little extra freshly ground black pepper
1 teaspoon (5 mL) dried thyme or basil leaves

METHOD

1. Follow the previous recipes to prepare the ingredients.

2. If you made the stew fresh, keep it hot by using the Sauté function as you prepare the dumplings.

3. If you are reheating the stew from the day before place it in a saucepan and bring it to a simmer.

4. Prepare the <u>dumplings</u> from one of the recipes on page 57

5. Putting the Hot Pot Together

1. Preheat your regular oven to 400°F (200°C, Gas Mark 6).

2. Ladle the steak and kidney stew filling equally between 4 broiler-safe French Onion soup bowls (or something similar - just make sure the dish is broiler-safe).

3. Gently drop the dumplings, using a large serving spoon, onto the hot steak and kidney stew until the entire top is covered.

4. Place the bowls on the upper rack of your oven (not right at the very top, we're not using the broiler but in the upper third).

5. Bake at 400°F (200°C, Gas Mark 6) for 25-30 minutes or until the dumplings are cooked through and the tops are brown and crusty.

6. Remove from the oven, allow to cool on a wire rack for 5-10 minutes, and serve.

Tip: You may want to arrange the Hot Pots on a cookie sheet before putting them in the oven. This makes it a little easier to get them in and out of the oven. Also, some of the dishes may bubble over, so it also contains any drips.

Tip: You can also make one large Hot Pot in a casserole dish, if you prefer. Just make sure the casserole dish is broiler safe.

CHEESY VEGETABLE HOT POT

A bit of a departure from the traditional Hot Pot. Instead of potatoes, this tasty dish is topped with breadcrumbs and a sharp Cheddar cheese.

INGREDIENTS FOR FILLING

1 tablespoon (15 mL) olive oil
2 medium yellow onions, halved and sliced
½ cup (120 mL) dry white wine
4 large carrots, peeled and cut into bite-size chunks
1 cup (75g) Crimini mushrooms, sliced (you can substitute white button mushrooms if you prefer)
1 small butternut squash, peeled and cut into bite-size chunks
1 teaspoon (5 mL) sea salt
½ teaspoon (2.5 mL) black pepper, freshly ground
1 tablespoon (15 mL) herbes de Provence
3 cups (700 mL) vegetable broth, preferably homemade (see page 17 - Stock)
2 tablespoons (30 mL) prepared whole grain brown mustard

INGREDIENTS FOR TOPPING

2 cups (100g) fresh breadcrumbs
1 cup (100g) sharp (mature) Cheddar cheese, grated

METHOD

Preparing the Hot Pot Filling

1. Select Sauté mode on your Instant Pot and allow the inner liner to heat up.

2. Once the inner pot is hot, add 1 tablespoon (15 mL) of the olive oil and allow it to heat up.

3. Add the onions and sauté for 2-3 minutes

4. Add the white wine and bring to a low simmer.

5. Use a wooden or silicone spatula to scrape any bits off the bottom of the pot.

6. Press Cancel to turn off Sauté mode.

7. Add the rest of the filling ingredients to the pot and stir well.

8. Close and lock the lid, ensuring that the Pressure Valve is in the Sealing position.

9. Select Manual/Pressure Cook mode and set the cooking time for 10 minutes. (Push the "+" or "-" buttons to set the required cooking time.)

10. When the cooking time is complete, allow a Natural Pressure Release for 10 minutes.

11. Turn the Pressure Valve to Venting to release any remaining pressure and, when the Float Valve has dropped, carefully open and remove the lid.

12. If the filling requires thickening, create a thin paste by combining, in a small bowl, approximately 1 tablespoon (15 mL) of cornstarch and enough water to create a pourable paste.

13. Select the Sauté button and allow the filling to come to a simmer.

14. Stir in the cornstarch mixture, a little at a time, until the desired thickness has been achieved. Then press Cancel to turn off Sauté mode.

Putting the Hot Pot Together
1. Ladle the filling equally between 4 broiler-safe French Onion soup bowls (or something similar - just make sure the dish is broiler-safe).

2. In a separate bowl, toss the breadcrumbs and grated cheese together.

3. Top each bowl with equal amounts of the cheese and breadcrumbs mixture and press slightly.

4. Broil for 5-10 minutes, or until the topping is brown and crispy.

5. Carefully remove the Hot Pots from the broiler and serve immediately.

Tip: You may want to arrange the Hot Pots on a cookie sheet before putting them in the broiler. This makes it a little easier to get them in and out of the oven. Also, some of the dishes may bubble over, so it also contains any drips.

Tip: You can also make one large Hot Pot in a casserole dish, if you prefer. Just make sure the casserole dish is broiler safe.

INSTANT POT RICE

Some of the recipes in this book suggest that they be served with rice. Here's a few ways you can make rice in your Instant Pot.

I have seen many posts online from people that have reported poor results cooking rice in their Instant Pot. I think the Instant Pot is the best rice cooker I've ever used.

You need to carefully follow the following directions for quantities of rice and water. Don't try to use the ratios you are used to - it won't work. The Instant Pot uses less water and less time than a stove top method.

Using the Instant Pot Automatic Rice Function for White Rice

Note: You can ONLY use the automatic Rice function for WHITE rice. Brown rice takes a lot longer to cook.

Note: This method will take at least 20 minutes total.

Ingredients

2 cups (450g) plain white rice, rinsed
2 cups (475 mL) water

Method

1. Place the rice and water in the inner liner of your Instant Pot and stir.

2. Be sure that the rice is completely immersed in the water and they're aren't any stray grains on the side of the pot.

3. Close and lock the lid ensuring the Pressure Valve is in the Sealing position.

4. Push the Rice button and let the Instant Pot do the rest.

5. When the cycle is complete do a Natural Release for 10 minutes and then release the rest of the pressure by carefully turning the Pressure Valve from Sealing to Venting.

6. Once all of the pressure has been released and the Float Valve has dropped, carefully open the lid.

7. Fluff the rice with a fork and serve.

   Tip: It's okay to do a total Natural Pressure Release on this setting, too.

Using Manual/Pressure Cook for White Rice

You can also use the Manual/Pressure Cook function for cooking white rice and it will be a lot faster than using the Rice function.

Ingredients

2 cups (450g) plain white rice, rinsed
2 cups (475 mL) water

Method

1. Place the rice and water in the inner liner of your Instant Pot and stir.

2. Be sure that the rice is completely immersed in the water and they're aren't any stray grains on the side of pot.

3. Close and lock the lid ensuring the Pressure Valve is in the Sealing position.

4. Select Manual/Pressure Cook mode and set the cooking time for 4 minutes. (Push the "+" or "-" buttons to set the required cooking time.)

5. When the cooking time is complete do a Natural Release for 10 minutes and then release the rest of the pressure by carefully turning the Pressure Valve from Sealing to Venting.

6. Once all of the pressure has been released and the Float Valve has dropped, carefully open the lid.

7. Fluff the rice with a fork and serve.

Using Manual/Pressure Cook
for Brown Rice

Brown rice takes longer to cook and you can't use the Rice function for brown rice.

Ingredients

2 cups (450g) brown rice, rinsed
2½ cups (600 mL) water

Method

1. Place the rice and water in the inner liner of your Instant Pot and stir.

2. Be sure that the rice is completely immersed in the water and they're aren't any stray grains on the side of the pot.

3. Close and lock the lid ensuring the Pressure Valve is in the Sealing position.

4. Select Manual/Pressure Cook mode and set the cooking time for 22 minutes. (Push the "+" or "-" buttons to set the required cooking time.)

5. When the cooking time is complete do a Natural Release for 10 minutes and then release the rest of the pressure by carefully turning the Pressure Valve from Sealing to Venting.

6. Once all of the pressure has been released and the Float Valve has dropped, carefully open the lid.

7. Fluff the rice with a fork and serve.

Cooking Rice Pot in Pot

When I want to do smaller amounts of rice, I like to cook them Pot in Pot (PIP). It's a lot easier to clean a smaller dish than the whole Instant Pot inner pot.

Here's what I do when I only want to cook a cup of brown rice.

Ingredients

1 cup (225g) brown rice, rinsed
1¼ cups (300 mL) water

Method

1. In an oven-safe dish that will fit easily inside your Instant Pot, combine the water and brown rice.

   Tip: I like to spray the dish with cooking spray so the rice doesn't stick.

2. Pour 1 cup (240 mL) water into the inner pot of your Instant and place the trivet in the pot as well.

3. Place the dish with the water and brown rice on top of the trivet.

   Note: There's no need to cover the dish because it's okay for the steam to come in contact with the rice.

4. Close and lock the lid ensuring the Pressure Valve is in the Sealing position.

5. Select Manual/Pressure Cook mode and set the cooking time for 22 minutes. (Push the "+" or "-" buttons to set the required cooking time.)

6. When the cooking time is complete do a Natural Release for 10 minutes and then release the rest of the pressure by carefully turning the Pressure Valve from Sealing to Venting.

7. Once all of the pressure has been released and the Float Valve has dropped, carefully open the lid.

8. Remove the dish with the rice in it to a heatproof surface.

9. Fluff the rice with a fork and serve.

CURRIES

Curries became very popular during the time of the British Empire and their popularity continues to this day.

Whenever you hear curry you naturally think of Indian food but today's curries are a mix of traditional Indian food and the Western influence.

Ginger, garlic, and turmeric were used for thousands of years but chili peppers (a prime ingredient in today's curry powder) didn't arrive in India until the 16th century.

Curry Powder As An Ingredient

A big problem when specifying curry powder in a recipe is that Curry Powder is a blend of many spices and the blend is not consistent.

I recommend you mix your own rather than buy a commercial blend or, at the very least you find a brand you like and stick to it.

Your Own Blend

I have included four suggested spice blends for your own curry powder but ideally, experiment to find just the mix that's right for you.

CURRY POWDER #1

This mixture uses whole seeds rather than ground spice. You grind it fresh when you use it.

INGREDIENTS

2 tablespoons (12g) whole cumin seeds, toasted
2 tablespoons (16g) whole cardamom pods, toasted
2 tablespoons (10g) whole coriander seeds, toasted
¼ cup (36g) ground turmeric
1 tablespoon (15 mL) dry mustard powder
1 teaspoon (5 mL) dry cayenne powder

METHOD

1. Place all ingredients in a container with an airtight lid.
2. Shake well to combine.
3. Can be stored in a cool dry place for up to 6 months.
4. Grind when ready to use and add to dishes according to taste.

Tip: A coffee grinder works well for grinding spices or use a pepper grinder filled with this mixture.

Curry Powder #2

This is a mild mixture but you can add more ground chilies if you like your curry hot.

Ingredients

- 2 tablespoons (12g) ground coriander
- 2 tablespoons (12g) ground cumin
- 1½ tablespoons (15g) ground turmeric
- 2 teaspoons (4g) ground ginger
- 1 teaspoon (5 mL) dry mustard powder
- ½ teaspoon (2.5 mL) ground black pepper
- 1 teaspoon (5 mL) ground cinnamon
- ½ teaspoon (2.5 mL) ground cardamom
- ½ teaspoon (2.5 mL) cayenne pepper or ground chilies

Method

1. Add all spices to a small jar and shake well.
2. Keep in a cool, dry place for up to 3 months.

CURRY POWDER #3

This mixture includes cloves and ginger.

INGREDIENTS

4½ teaspoons (22.5 mL) ground coriander

2 teaspoons (10 mL) ground turmeric

1½ teaspoons (7.5 mL) ground cumin

½ teaspoon (2.5 mL) ground black pepper

½ teaspoon (2.5 mL) ground cayenne pepper

½ teaspoon (2.5 mL) ground cardamom

¼ teaspoon (1.25 mL) ground cinnamon

¼ teaspoon (1.25 mL) ground cloves

¼ teaspoon (1.25 mL) ground ginger

METHOD

1. Add all spices to a small jar and shake well.
2. Keep in a cool, dry place for up to 3 months.

Curry Powder #4 - Thai

Try this mixture if you want to get a Thai curry flavour.

Ingredients

1 tablespoon (15 mL) ground turmeric
3 tablespoons (45 mL) ground coriander
2 tablespoons (30 mL) ground cumin
2 teaspoons (10 mL) ground ginger
1 teaspoon (5 mL) ground white pepper
1 to 3 teaspoons (5 to 15 mL) cayenne pepper (according to preference)
⅛ teaspoon (0.625 mL) ground cloves

Method

1. Add all spices to a small jar and shake well.

2. Keep in a cool, dry place for up to 3 months.

3. When using this Curry powder, add 1 or 2 bay leaves when cooking your curry.

Bonus Recipe: Naan Bread

Traditionally, naan bread is cooked in a Tandoor (a cylindrical metal, or clay, oven used in Southern, Central and Western Asia). However, it can also be made, quite successfully, in your own kitchen.

It's a flat bread that is popular in East Indian cuisine.

Ingredients

¾ cup (180 mL) whole milk, warmed to approximately 80° F.

¾ cup (180 mL) plain yogurt

1 large egg

2 tablespoons (30 mL) extra virgin olive oil

2 teaspoons (10 mL) sugar

1 teaspoon (5 mL) sea salt

4 cups (480 g) unbleached all-purpose flour

1 teaspoon (5 mL) baking powder

2 teaspoons (10 mL) active dry yeast

Method

1. Place all of the ingredients in the pan of your bread machine in the order suggested by the manufacturer. (I have listed the ingredients in the order that I use in my bread machine.)

2. Select the dough setting.

3. As the dough is mixing, check to see if you need to add a little more flour or a little more water to get the correct consistency of dough.

4. Once the dough is ready, turn it out onto a lightly floured surface and knead slightly.

5. At this point, it's a good idea to weigh the dough to be able to determine the size of each ball of dough. From this recipe, the dough weighed 2 lbs 8 oz or 40 oz. (1.1 Kg)

6. Divide the dough into 8 - 5 oz (142g) pieces and roll each piece into a ball.

7. On a lightly floured surface, flattened out each ball, one at a time, and, using a rolling pin, roll each ball into a flat oval, approximately ¼" thick and let rest for 5 minutes.

8. While the dough is resting, heat a heavy skillet on medium high heat and grease the pan. (I like to use coconut oil for this.)

9. When the pan is hot, brush one side of an oval with water and place it in the hot, greased skillet, water side down.

10. Cover the skillet and cook for 1 minute. (Note: the naan may create some air bubbles and that's okay.)

11. Turn the naan, cover the skillet again, and cook for another minute.

12. The naan should be nicely browned on both sides.

13. Transfer to a warm plate and cover with a tea towel.

14. Repeat with each piece of dough, replenishing the coconut oil as needed, until all of the pieces have been cooked.

15. If you plan to serve the naan immediately, you can brush each piece with clarified butter (ghee) and sprinkle with herbs or spices of your choice.

16. If you're not planning to use the naan right away, skip that step.

Naan freezes very well and can be reheated by allowing it to thaw and then rewarming it in a lightly greased, heated skillet. I've also had success putting the thawed naan bread in a toaster.

Chicken Vindaloo

Brits love their curries, but each time I cook a Vindaloo I can't help but think of that amazing British series, Red Dwarf. Dave Lister just loved his Vindaloo!

Ingredients

1 pound (454g) boneless, skinless chicken thighs
1 medium yellow onion, halved and sliced
4-6 whole red dried chilies (for a milder flavor, de-seed the chilies before soaking them)
½ inch (1.25 cm) piece of ginger, peeled, sliced and minced
4 cloves garlic, minced
1 tablespoon (15 mL) garam masala
3 tablespoons (45 mL) red wine vinegar
1 teaspoon (5 mL) turmeric powder
1 teaspoon (5 mL) sea salt
1 teaspoon (5 mL) granulated sugar
2 teaspoons (10 mL) olive oil
1 medium carrot, peeled and diced
1 cup (325g) cauliflower florets

Garnish

chopped fresh cilantro for garnish (optional)

Method

1. In a separate bowl, soak the dry chilies in ½ cup hot water for approximately 10 minutes.
2. Select Sauté mode on your Instant Pot and allow it to heat up.
3. Add the olive oil and allow it to heat up.
4. Add the onions and sauté for 1-2 minutes.
5. Press Cancel to turn off Sauté mode.

6. In a food processor or blender, combine the onions, soaked chilies and the liquid, all the dry spices, salt and sugar. Purée to achieve a smooth paste.

7. To the inner pot of your Instant Pot, add the spice purée, ½ cup (120 mL) water, the chicken thighs and mix well.

8. Close and lock the lid, ensuring that the Pressure Valve is in the Sealing position.

9. Select Manual/Pressure Cook mode and set the cooking time for 6 minutes. (Push the "+" or "-" buttons to set the required cooking time.)

10. Once the cooking time is complete, allow a Natural Pressure Release.

11. Once the Float Valve has dropped on its own, carefully open and remove the lid.

12. Add the carrots and cauliflower and mix well.

13. Close and lock the lid, ensuring that the Pressure Valve is in the Sealing position.

14. Select Manual/Pressure Cook mode and set the cooking time for 2 minutes. (Push the "+" or "-" buttons to set the required cooking time.)

15. When the cooking time is complete, do a Quick Release by carefully turning the Pressure Valve from Sealing to Venting.

16. Serve over rice and sprinkle with chopped Cilantro, if desired.

   Note: See the bonus instructions for Instant Pot brown or white rice.

FISH & COCONUT CURRY

In this recipe we're going to be using Curry leaves (or kaffir lime leaves as a substitute). This is not the same as curry powder. Curry powder is not made from curry leaves, but rather a blend of spices. However, curry leaves are often used in Indian cooking.

You may be able to find curry leaves (or kaffir lime leaves) in your local grocery store in the Asian section. If not, check our website for suggestions. (https://ebooks.geezerguides.com/products-from-our-books/)

INGREDIENTS

1 tablespoon (15 mL) olive oil
½ teaspoon (2.5 mL) mustard seeds
10 - 15 curry leaves (or 2 - 3 kaffir lime leaves)
½ inch (1.25 cm) piece of ginger, peeled, sliced and minced
4 cloves garlic, minced
1 medium yellow onion, halved and sliced
½ green bell pepper, sliced
½ orange or yellow bell pepper, sliced
1 teaspoon (5 mL) sea salt
½ teaspoon (2.5 mL) turmeric powder
½ teaspoon (2.5 mL) red chili powder (or to taste)
2 teaspoons (10 mL) ground coriander
1 teaspoon (5 mL) ground cumin
1 teaspoon (5 mL) garam masala
1 teaspoon (5 mL) fresh cilantro, chopped (optional)
1 - 13.5 ounce (400 mL) can coconut milk
1 pound (454g) firm white fish, cut in 2 inch (5 cm) pieces and patted dry
½ teaspoon (2.5 mL) lime juice, freshly squeezed if possible

GARNISH

toasted coconut flakes for garnish (optional)

METHOD

1. Select Sauté mode on your Instant Pot and allow it to heat up.

2. Add the olive oil and allow it to heat up.

3. Add the mustard seeds and sauté for about 30 seconds.

4. Add the curry leaves (or kaffir leaves) and sauté for an additional 30 seconds.

5. Add the onions and bell peppers and sauté for about 1 minute.

6. Add all spices, stir well and sauté another 30 seconds.

7. Add coconut milk, mix well and bring it to a simmer for about a minute. Doing this will help prevent the coconut milk from curdling while it is under pressure.

8. Press Cancel to turn off Sauté mode.

9. Add the fish and stir gently, being sure that the fish is well coated.

10. Close and lock the lid, ensuring that the Pressure Valve is in the Sealing position.

11. Select Manual/Pressure Cook mode and set the cooking time for 3 minutes. (Push the "+" or "-" buttons to set the required cooking time.)

12. Once the cooking time is complete, do a Quick Release by carefully turning the Pressure Valve from the Sealing position to the Venting position.

13. When all the pressure has been released, and the Float Valve has dropped, carefully remove the lid.

14. Add the lime juice, give it a quick stir and serve over rice and garnish with toasted coconut flakes, if desired.

Beef Vindaloo

Yes, we Brits love our Indian-inspired dishes, so here's another Vindaloo.

This recipe calls for a few more "exotic" ingredients. You should be able to find most of the these in the Asian section of your grocery store or in a specialty store. If not, check out our website for suggestions. (https://ebooks.geezerguides.com/products-from-our-books/)

Ingredients

Marinade Ingredients

½ teaspoon (2.5 mL) ground cinnamon
¼ teaspoon (1.25 mL) ground cloves
1 teaspoon (5 mL) amchoor powder, sometimes known as mango powder (or substitute lemon or lime juice)
1 teaspoon (5 mL) ground turmeric
½ teaspoon (2.5 mL) ground cumin
2 tablespoons (30 mL) mild red chili powder
½ teaspoon (2.5 mL) black pepper, freshly ground
½ cup (50g) yellow onion, chopped
8 cloves garlic, chopped
½ cup (25g) fresh ginger, peeled and chopped
1 tablespoon (15 mL) lemon juice
1 teaspoon (5 mL) coarse sea salt or coarse Himalayan pink salt
1 teaspoon (5 mL) liquid honey
3 tablespoons (45 mL) tamarind paste
¼ cup (60 mL) white vinegar

Add beef to marinade

10-12 cardamom pods, crushed
2 pounds (500g) beef shank (shin), cut into bite-size pieces

Add final ingredients

2 tablespoons (30 mL) olive oil
1 cup (100g) yellow onions, halved and sliced

2 green chili peppers, sliced (choose a green chili pepper according to your taste, and the amount of "heat" you prefer, eg. jalapeño, Anaheim, Cayenne, etc.)
2 large, ripe tomatoes, chopped
1 cup (240 mL) beef broth, preferably homemade (see page 17 - Stock)

METHOD

Making the Marinated Beef

1. Add all of the marinade ingredients to a blender and blend everything to a paste.

2. In a medium bowl, combine the blended marinade, the crushed cardamom pods and the bite-size beef. Toss to make sure the beef is well covered.

3. Cover and marinate in your refrigerator for at least 12 - 24 hours.

Cooking in your Instant Pot

1. Select Sauté mode and allow the inner pot to heat up.

2. Add the olive oil and allow it to heat up.

3. Add the onions and sauté for 3-4 minutes.

4. Add the beef, with the marinade and sauté for 3-4 minutes.

5. Add the rest of the ingredients and stir well.

6. Press Cancel to turn off Sauté mode.

7. Close and lock the lid, ensuring the Pressure Valve is in the Sealing position.

8. Select Meat/Stew mode and set the cooking time for 35 minutes. (Push the "+" or "-" buttons to set the required cooking time.)

9. Once the cooking time is complete, allow a Natural Pressure Release.

10. Once the Float Valve has dropped on its own, carefully open and remove the lid.

11. Remove the beef with a slotted spoon and keep warm.

12. Select Sauté mode and bring the sauce to a simmer. Simmer until the sauce has thickened (approximately 10 minutes).

13. Press Cancel to turn off Sauté mode and return the beef to the sauce.

14. Stir well and serve.

Mock Tandoori Chicken

Even though this tastes just like Tandoori Chicken, we can't call it that. After all, the Instant Pot is not a Tandoor, but it sure makes a Tandoori Chicken taste-alike!

Ingredients

Marinade Ingredients
1 to 2 teaspoon (5 to 10 mL) red chili powder, or to taste
½ teaspoon (2.5 mL) turmeric powder
2 teaspoons (10 mL) ginger powder or 2 tablespoons (30 mL) freshly grated ginger
2 teaspoons (10 mL) garlic powder
2 teaspoons (10 mL) ground coriander
Juice of 1 whole lemon
½ teaspoon (2.5 mL) sea salt

Add chicken to marinade
2 pounds (900g) boneless, skinless chicken breast or thighs (or combination), cut chicken breasts in half (if using) and leave thighs whole

Add final ingredients
2 tablespoons (30 mL) olive oil
1 teaspoon (5 mL) coriander seeds
1 large yellow onion, halved and sliced
1 teaspoon (5 mL) freshly grated ginger
3 cloves garlic, minced
2 teaspoons (10 mL) garam masala
1 teaspoon (5 mL) red chili powder
2 medium tomatoes, cored and chopped
½ cup (120 mL) chicken or vegetable broth, preferably homemade (see page 17 - Stock)
1 teaspoon (5 mL) sea salt (or to taste)

Garnish
Fresh cilantro leaves chopped, for garnish

METHOD

Marinating the Chicken

1. In a medium bowl, combine all the marinade ingredients and mix well.

2. Add the chicken, toss well and then rub the marinade into the chicken.

3. Cover and keep in the refrigerator for an hour.

Cooking in the Instant Pot

1. Select Sauté mode and let the inner pot heat up.

2. Add the olive oil and allow it to heat up.

3. Add the coriander seeds and heat until several of them begin to "pop".

4. Add the onion and sauté for 3-4 minutes.

5. Add the rest of the spices, stir well and sauté for another 30 seconds to 1 minute.

6. Add the tomatoes and sauté for a minute or two.

7. Add the chicken and sauté for a minute or two.

8. Add the broth and use a wooden or silicone spatula to scrape any bits off the bottom of the pot.

9. Press Cancel to turn off Sauté mode.

10. Close and lock the lid, ensuring that the Pressure Valve is in the Sealing position.

11. Select Poultry mode and set the cooking time for 8 minutes. (Push the "+" or "-" buttons to set the required cooking time.)

12. Once the cooking time is complete, allow a Natural Pressure Release for 10 minutes, then carefully release the rest of the pressure manually.

13. Once all the pressure has been released and the Float Valve has dropped, carefully open and remove the lid.

14. Place one or two pieces of chicken (depending on size) on each plate, spoon the sauce over them and sprinkle with the chopped cilantro, if desired.

15. If you are serving with rice, you can also spoon some of the sauce over the rice.

CHICKEN CURRY SOUP

Sometimes you just want a little extra spiciness to your chicken soup and this recipe does just that, as well as adding a nice creaminess, too.

INGREDIENTS

2 tablespoons (30 mL) olive oil
1 cup (150g) yellow onion, chopped
2 tablespoons (30 mL) garlic, minced
2 tablespoons (30 mL) fresh ginger, peeled and finely chopped
1 jalapeño pepper, sliced (optional)
Note: remove the seeds for a milder flavor

2 tablespoons (30 mL) curry powder, or to taste depending on the strength of your curry powder
1½ teaspoons (7.5 mL) sea salt (or to taste)
Note: you may want to omit the salt if you're using a commercial broth

1 teaspoon (5 mL) black pepper, freshly ground
2 pounds (900g) boneless skinless chicken thighs, cut into bite-size pieces
4 cups (950 mL) chicken broth, preferably homemade (see page 17 - Stock)
1 cup (240 mL) canned diced tomatoes
Add final ingredients
3 cups (675g) fresh baby spinach
1 cup (240 mL) coconut milk
¼ cup (15g) fresh cilantro, chopped, optional

METHOD

1. Select Sauté mode and allow the inner pot of your Instant Pot to heat up.
2. Add the olive oil and allow it to heat up.
3. Add the onions and sauté for 1-2 minutes.

4. Add the garlic, ginger and jalapeño and sauté for about 1 minute.

5. Add the curry powder, salt and pepper and stir.

   Note: You don't want to let the spices burn. Add a little broth if necessary.

6. Add the chicken and stir well so it gets coated with the spice mixture.

7. Add the broth and use a wooden or silicone spatula to scrape any bits from the bottom of the pan.

8. Add the tomatoes and stir well.

9. Press Cancel to turn off Sauté mode.

10. Close and lock the lid, ensuring that the Pressure Valve is in the Sealing position.

11. Select Manual/Pressure Cook mode and set the cooking time for 6 minutes. (Push the "+" or "-" buttons to set the required cooking time.)

12. Once the cooking time is complete, allow a Natural Pressure Release.

13. Once the Float Valve has dropped on its own, carefully open and remove the lid.

14. Add the spinach and coconut milk.

15. Select Sauté mode and cook until the spinach wilts and soup is heated through.

16. Press Cancel to turn off Sauté mode.

17. Stir in the cilantro, if using, and serve.

Chicken Tikka Masala

Marinade Ingredients

1 cup (240 mL) plain Greek yogurt

1 tablespoon (15 mL) garam masala

1 tablespoon (15 mL) lemon juice, preferably freshly squeezed

1 teaspoon (5 mL) black pepper, freshly ground

1 inch (2.5 cm) fresh ginger, peeled and finely minced

Add the chicken

1 pound (450g) boneless skinless chicken breasts, cut in bite-size pieces

Sauce Ingredients

1 tablespoon (15 mL) olive oil

1 small yellow onion, halved and sliced

5 cloves garlic, minced

4 teaspoons (20 mL) garam masala

½ teaspoon (2.5 mL) paprika

½ teaspoon (2.5 mL) turmeric

½ teaspoon (2.5 mL) sea salt

¼ teaspoon (1.25 mL) cayenne

2 cups (475 mL) tomato sauce

Add final ingredient

1 cup (240 mL) full fat coconut milk

Method

Marinating

1. In a medium non-reactive bowl (such as glass), combine all of the marinade ingredients and mix well.

2. Add the chicken and mix well to make sure the chicken is well coated.

3. Cover and refrigerate for at least one hour.

Cooking

1. Select Sauté mode on your Instant pot and allow it to heat up.

2. Add the olive oil and allow it to heat up.

3. Add the onions and garlic and sauté for 2-3 minutes.

4. Add the chicken chunks with whatever marinade sticks to them and discard the rest of the marinade.

5. Cook the chicken chunks for 2-3 minutes, stirring frequently so they get sautéed on all sides.

6. Add the spices and sauté for about a minute.

7. Press Cancel to turn off Sauté mode.

8. Add the tomato sauce and use a wooden or silicone spatula to scrape any bits off the bottom of the pan.

9. Close and lock the lid, ensuring that the Pressure Valve is in the Sealing position.

10. Select Manual/Pressure Cook mode and set cooking time for 10 minutes. (Push the "+" or "-" buttons to set the required cooking time.)

11. Once cooking time is complete do a Quick Release by carefully turning the Pressure Valve from Sealing to Venting.

12. When all of the pressure has been released, and the Float Valve has dropped, carefully open the lid.

13. Select Sauté mode and stir in the coconut milk.

14. Continue stirring until the sauce thickens to the desired consistency (about 5-10 minutes).

15. Serve immediately with a rice of your choice.

    Tip: You can also sprinkle this dish with some chopped fresh cilantro, if desired.

Beef Curry

A good hearty beef curry is lovely served with potatoes or rice and a vegetable or two of your choice. A side of freshly made Naan bread wouldn't go amiss, either. (see recipe on page 120).

Ingredients

1 tablespoon (15 mL) olive oil
2 medium yellow onions, halved and sliced
3-4 cloves garlic, minced
1 teaspoon (5 mL) ground cumin
1 teaspoon (5 mL) mustard seeds
1 teaspoon (5 mL) ground turmeric
1 teaspoon (5 mL) garam masala
½ inch (1.25 cm) fresh ginger, peeled and minced
2 red chili peppers, chopped (for a milder taste, you can substitute jalapeño peppers)
2 pounds (900g) beef, such as chuck, cut into bite-size pieces
1 cup (240 mL) beef broth, preferably homemade (see page 17 - Stock)
2 cups (475 mL) diced tomatoes, fresh or canned
2 tablespoons (30 mL) tomato paste
½ cup (100g) red lentils (optional, but recommended for thickening and taste)

Garnish

½ cup (25 g) chopped fresh cilantro for garnish (optional)

Method:

1. Select Sauté mode and allow the inner pot to heat up.

2. Add the olive oil and allow it to heat up.

3. Add the onions and garlic and sauté for 1-2 minutes.

4. Add the spices and pepper (if using) and sauté for about 1 minute.

5. Add the beef and stir until it is slightly brown on all sides.

6. Add the beef broth and use a wooden or silicone spatula to scrape any bits from the bottom of the pot.

7. Add the tomatoes, tomato paste and lentils. Stir well.

8. Close and lock the lid ensuring that the Pressure Valve is in the Sealing position.

9. Select Meat/Stew mode and set the cooking time for 20 minutes. (Push the "+" or "-" buttons to set the required cooking time.)

10. Once cooking time is complete, allow a Natural Pressure Release. That means letting the pressure go down naturally and waiting for the Float Valve to drop on its own.

11. Once the Float Valve has dropped, carefully open the lid.

12. If the sauce needs thickening, turn on Sauté mode and bring the curry to a simmer. Mix approximately 1 tablespoon (15 mL) of cornstarch with just enough water to make a pourable paste.

13. While the curry is simmering, slowly pour in the cornstarch mixture, stirring constantly.

14. When the desired consistency is reached, press Cancel to turn off Sauté mode and serve immediately.

15. Sprinkle with chopped cilantro, if desired.

Spinach and Chickpea Curry

This is a super-easy vegetarian/vegan curry that starts with dried chickpeas, not pre-cooked or canned. It can be served with rice, quinoa or potatoes.

Ingredients

2 tablespoons (30 mL) olive oil
1 small red onion, halved and sliced
2 cloves garlic, minced
½ teaspoon (2.5 mL) chili powder
½ teaspoon (2.5 mL) garam masala
1 tablespoon (15 mL) curry powder
2 bay leaves
1½ cups (300g) dried chickpeas, rinsed
1½ cups (350 mL) vegetable broth, preferably homemade (see page 17 - Stock)
1 cup (240 mL) canned crushed tomatoes
1 teaspoon (5 mL) sea salt
½ teaspoon (2.5 mL) black pepper, freshly ground

Add final ingredients

1 - 2 tablespoons (15 - 30 mL) lemon juice, freshly squeezed if possible
10 ounces (285g) baby spinach, packed

Garnish

Chopped cilantro for garnish (optional)

Method

1. Select Sauté mode and allow the inner pot to heat up.
2. Add the olive oil and allow it to heat up.
3. Add the onion and garlic and sauté for 2-3 minutes
4. Add the spices and sauté for another minute.
5. Add the chickpeas and toss well to coat with the spices.
6. Add the vegetable broth and use a wooden or silicone spatula to scrape any bits from the bottom of the pot.

7. Add the crushed tomatoes, salt and pepper and stir well.

8. Press Cancel to turn off Sauté mode.

9. Close and lock the lid ensuring the Pressure Valve is in the Sealing position.

10. Select Bean/Chili mode and set the cooking time for 35 minutes. (Push the "+" or "-" buttons to set the required cooking time.)

11. Once cooking time is complete, allow a Natural Pressure Release. That means letting the pressure go down naturally and waiting for the Float Valve to drop on its own.

12. Once the Float Valve has dropped, carefully open the lid.

13. Select Sauté mode and bring the liquid to a low simmer.

14. Add the lemon juice and baby spinach, stirring just until the spinach wilts.

15. Press the Cancel button to turn off Sauté mode.

16. Serve immediately and sprinkle with chopped cilantro, if desired.

STEAMED PUDDINGS

Steamed puddings are delicious but do tend to be a little heavy. I don't recommend you eat them regularly but for special occasions it's certainly something a little different you can prepare to impress your guests.

Instant Pot Steamed Puddings

The advantages of using the Instant Pot to cook a steamed pudding are that it saves a little time and you don't have to constantly monitor the water level.

I love steamed puddings, in fact steak and kidney pudding is probably my most favorite meal of all. And my wife and I are now mostly vegetarian. I'm not worried about the suet but we do try to avoid eating meat most of the time.

One of the drawbacks to eating a steamed pudding is that they are a bit of a pain to cook using the stove top method. You have to keep a close eye on the water level in case you run out or overflow the basin.

The Instant Pot eliminates this drawback and makes cooking suet puddings very easy. They are still not diet food but they certainly make for an occasional treat and are sure to be a hit with your dinner party guest who have probably never tried one before.

*Substitutes for Suet

Real suet can be difficult to find in North America. If you are not able to obtain real suet you can substitute:

❖ the same amount of lard, frozen and shredded or

❖ the same amount of vegetable shortening, frozen and shredded or

❖ a package of Atora™ from Amazon - look on our website for a link - https://ebooks.geezerguides.com/products-from-our-books/

140

Basic Suet Crust

A suet crust is just a type of pastry but instead of baking it in an oven you boil or steam it. The result is more like a dumpling than a pie crust. In fact what I consider "real" dumplings are always made with suet. If you normally use Bisquik® for your dumplings give my suet dumpling recipe a try.

Suet pudding is a delicious English tradition found in both meat and fruit dishes. It can be eaten as is or covered with various toppings depending on whether you are preparing an entrée or a dessert.

The basic recipe for a suet crust is 1 part suet to 1½ parts flour. Since this is self-raising flour you will need to add 1½ teaspoons of baking powder and ¼ teaspoon of salt to every cup of all purpose flour.

A Few Tips

There are a few tips I want to share that will help make your suet puddings as good as they can be.

Start with your suet at room temperature. In other words take it out of the fridge an hour or so before you begin using it.

Suet pastry expands quite a bit as it cooks so be sure to allow for this. Fill pudding basins only two-thirds full to allow room for expansion.

How to Steam Using an Instant Pot?

We now use an Instant Pot whenever we make a steamed pudding. It's just easier and more convenient than the stove top method.

It's also much faster and we don't have to worry about constantly checking the water level.

Savoury Suet Pastry

Use this recipe for all your savoury meat and cheese puddings. Use ¾ of the dough to line the bottom and sides of your basin and the remaining ¼ for the pastry lid.

Ingredients

 1½ cups (180g) flour
 1 tablespoon (15 mL) baking powder
 ¾ teaspoon(4 mL salt)
 ¼ teaspoon (1.25 mL) pepper
 1 cup (125g) suet
 8 - 10 tablespoons (40-50 mL) cold water

Method

In a medium bowl, mix together the flour, baking powder, salt and pepper. Mix well with a fork to make sure the ingredients are well combined.

Cut in the suet, using a pastry blender, until the mixture looks like a coarse meal.

Trickle the cold water over the dry ingredients and mix with a fork until it begins to form a dough. Then, knead the dough until it is well formed and still a little sticky.

Sweet Suet Pastry

Use this recipe for all your sweet and fruit puddings. For filled fruit pudding use ¾ of the dough to line the bottom and sides of your basin and the remaining ¼ for the pastry lid.

If you're making a rolled pudding like a Spotted Dick or Roly-poly, roll the pastry to a rectangle approximately 7 inches (17.5 cm) by 14 inches (35.5 cm). Add your filling and roll up to form an 7 inches (17.5 cm) finished length.

Ingredients

    1½ cups (180 g) all purpose flour
    ⅓ cup (65g) sugar
    1 tablespoon (15 mL) baking powder
    ¾ teaspoon (4 mL) salt
    1 cup (125g) suet, finely chopped
    8 - 10 tablespoons (40-50 mL) milk

Method

In a medium bowl, mix together the flour, sugar, baking powder and salt. Mix well with a fork to make sure the ingredients are well combined.

Cut in the suet, using a pastry blender, until the mixture looks like a coarse meal.

Trickle the milk over the dry ingredients and mix with a fork until it begins to form a dough. Then, knead the dough until it is well formed and still a little sticky.

Spotted Dick

There are many recipes around for Spotted Dick and some of them suggest you make this recipe in a basin, like other steamed puddings. However, that is NOT a traditional Spotted Dick.

This recipe is for a traditional Spotted Dick cooked in a non-traditional way - in an Instant Pot! And that's the only way this recipe differs from the traditional recipe.

Ingredients

1 recipe sweet suet pastry (see page 143)

Choose Filling #1

¾ cup (115g) currants
1 small cooking apple, peeled, cored and diced
⅓ cup (60g) brown sugar
½ large lemon, zest only

or Choose Filling #2

¼ cup (40g) currants
¼ cup (40g) craisins (dried cranberries)
¼ cup (30g) walnuts
¼ cup (40g) dried mixed fruit
⅓ cup (60g) brown sugar, packed

or Create Your Own Filling

It's okay to experiment. As long as you keep the quantities about the same you can mix up the filling ingredients. For example, I used raisins instead of currants, chopped almonds instead of walnuts, some chopped candied peel instead of the dried mix fruit ... you get the idea.

Method

1. In a medium bowl, mix all the filling ingredients together making sure that the brown sugar is well distributed throughout the fruit and nuts. Set aside.

2. On a lightly floured surface, roll out the sweet suet pastry to form a rectangle approximately 6½ to 7 inches (16.5 to 17.5 cm) by 10 to 11 inches (25 to 28 cm).

3. Evenly distribute the filling over the pastry and press the filling lightly into the pastry.

4. Roll up the pastry, as tightly as possible, from the smaller end. For example, start from the edge that is 6½ to 7 inches (16.5 to 17.5 cm) wide so when you are finished you have a Spotted Dick that is 6½ to 7 inches (16.5 to 17.5 cm) long.

5. Seal the ends and the seam by pinching them together.

6. Wrap the Spotted Dick well in 2 or 3 layers of aluminum foil and twist the ends to seal.

7. Place the trivet in the inner liner and pour in 2 cups (480 mL) of boiling water.

8. Carefully place the foil-wrapped pudding on the trivet.

9. Close and lock the lid of the Instant Pot, ensuring the Pressure Valve is in the Sealing position.

10. Select the Steam function and set the cooking time for 45 minutes.

11. Once cooking time is complete allow for a complete Natural Pressure Release (Wait for the float valve to drop on its own. This can take up to 45 minutes.)

12. Remove the completed Spotted Dick from the Instant Pot and allow to cool on a wire rack for 5-10 minutes.

13. Carefully remove the aluminum foil and slice into serving portions.

14. Serve with Tate & Lyle's Golden Syrup or Bird's custard.

Apple and Blackberry Pudding

Ingredients

1 recipe <u>sweet suet pastry</u> (see page 143)

Filling

2 large cooking apples, cored, peeled and sliced
1½ cups (190g) blackberries
⅓ cup (65g) sugar

Method

1. Roll out the sweet suet pastry and line a 1½ pint (700 mL) pudding basin with three-quarters of the pastry, reserving one-quarter for the lid.

   Note: make sure the pudding basin will fit properly in your Instant Pot.

2. In a medium bowl, toss together the apple slices, blackberries and sugar. Ladle the fruit and sugar mixture into the pastry-lined pudding basin.

3. Wet the edges of the pastry lid and then pinch the edges to seal the lid.

4. Cover the top of the pudding basin with parchment paper or aluminum foil and a pudding cloth. Tie the pudding cloth securely with string and gather any excess pudding cloth over the top of the basin.

   Note: The pudding cloth is optional, however, you need to make sure that no water gets into the basin while it's steaming. I like to use a pudding cloth because that's the way I've always done it. And, it makes it easier to get the pudding into and out of the pot.

5. Place the trivet in the stainless steel liner of the Instant Pot.

6. Add approximately 6 cups (1.4 L) of boiling water to the inner pot (This worked perfect for the basin I used in a 6-quart Instant Pot. The goal is to have the water be about 1" (2.5 cm) below the rim of the pudding basin. Adjust the amount of boiling water to suit your pot and basin.)

7. Gently lower the prepared pudding basin onto the trivet. Check the water level in relation to the pudding basin and adjust if necessary.

8. Close and lock the lid of the Instant Pot, ensuring the Pressure Valve is in the Sealing position.

9. Select the Steam function and set the cooking time for 90 minutes.

10. Once cooking time is complete allow for a complete Natural Pressure Release (Wait for the float valve to drop on its own. This can take up to 45 minutes.)

11. Remove the completed pudding from the Instant Pot and carefully remove the pudding cloth and parchment paper or aluminum foil.

12. Allow the pudding to cool for 10-15 minutes.

13. Invert on a serving dish, if desired.

14. Serve with Bird's custard, heavy cream or ice cream.

Carrot-Raisin Pudding

Ingredients

2 medium carrots, coarsely grated
2 medium apples, peeled, cored and finely chopped
1 medium potato, peeled and finely chopped
1 cup (125g) suet, chopped (see page 140 for alternatives)
1 cup (200g) sugar
⅓ cup (80 mL) orange juice
1 egg, beaten
1 teaspoon (5 mL) vanilla
1½ cups (180g) all purpose flour
1½ teaspoons (7.5 mL) baking soda
1 teaspoon (5 mL) cinnamon
1 teaspoon (5 mL) nutmeg, freshly grated
½ teaspoon (2.5 mL) ground cloves
½ teaspoon (2.5 mL) salt
1 cup (175g) dates, chopped
1 cup (150g) raisins

Method

1. Grease a 2 pint (950 mL) pudding basin

   Note: make sure the pudding basin will fit properly in your Instant Pot.

2. In a large bowl, combine the carrots, apples, potato and suet. Mix well.

3. In a large measuring cup, combine the sugar, orange juice, egg, and vanilla. Mix well and stir into the carrot mixture.

4. In a medium bowl, combine the flour, baking soda, cinnamon, nutmeg, cloves, and salt. Mix well and stir into the carrot mixture.

5. Fold the dates and raisins into the carrot mixture.

6. Pour the batter into the greased pudding basin.

7. Cover the top of the pudding basin with parchment paper or aluminum foil and a pudding cloth. Tie the pudding cloth securely with string and gather any excess pudding cloth over the top of the basin.

   Note: The pudding cloth is optional, however, you need to make sure that no water gets into the basin while it's steaming. I like to use a pudding cloth because that's the way I've always done it. And, it makes it easier to get the pudding into and out of the pot.

8. Place the trivet in the stainless steel liner of the Instant Pot.

9. Add approximately 6 cups (1.4 L) of boiling water to the inner pot (This worked perfect for the basin I used in a 6-quart Instant Pot. The goal is to have the water be about 1" (2.5 cm) below the rim of the pudding basin. Adjust the amount of boiling water to suit your pot and basin.)

10. Gently lower the prepared pudding basin onto the trivet. Check the water level in relation to the pudding basin and adjust if necessary.

11. Close and lock the lid of the Instant Pot, ensuring the Pressure Valve is in the Sealing position.

12. Select the Steam function and set the cooking time for 120 minutes.

13. Once cooking time is complete allow for a complete Natural Pressure Release (Wait for the float valve to drop on its own. This can take up to 45 minutes.)

14. Remove the completed pudding from the Instant Pot and carefully remove the pudding cloth and parchment paper or aluminum foil.

15. Allow the pudding to cool for 10-15 minutes.

16. Invert on a serving dish, if desired.

17. Serve with Bird's custard, heavy cream or ice cream.

Christmas Plum Pudding

This recipe makes a lot - enough for 4 to 6 steamed puddings depending on the size of basin (bowl) you choose to use - 1½ or 2 pint (700 or 900 mL). You'll need to cook each one individually in the Instant Pot.

Ingredients

1¼ cups (150g) all purpose flour
½ teaspoon (2.5 mL) baking soda
1 teaspoon (5 mL) salt
1¼ cups (190g) Sultana raisins
1¼ cups (190g) seedless raisins
1 cup (150g) currants
1 cup (75g) mixed peel, chopped
1 cup (95g) maraschino cherries
1 cup (110g) blanched almonds, chopped
2 tablespoons (15g) all purpose flour
½ cup (115g) butter
1¼ cups (225g) brown sugar, firmly packed
4 eggs, beaten
2 tablespoons (30 mL) molasses
1½ cups (135g) dry bread crumbs
½ cup (120 mL) brandy
1 teaspoon (5 mL) cinnamon
½ teaspoon (2.5 mL) nutmeg
½ teaspoon (2.5 mL) ground cloves
1½ cups (185g) suet, finely chopped (see page 140 for alternatives)
⅔ cup (160 mL) milk

Method

1. In a medium bowl or measuring cup, combine the flour, baking soda and salt. Set aside.

2. In a medium bowl, mix together the raisins, currants, peel, cherries, nuts and 2 tablespoons (15g) of flour. Toss well so that the flour coats all the other ingredients. Set aside.

150

3. In a large bowl cream together the butter and brown sugar until light and fluffy.

4. Beat the eggs well and add to the butter and sugar mixture. Then add the molasses, bread crumbs, brandy, spices and suet. Mix well.

5. Add in the floured fruit and nut mixture and mix well.

6. Add the flour, baking soda and salt mixture alternately with the milk and mix well.

7. Grease the pudding molds well and fill about ⅔rds full as the puddings will rise.

8. Cover the top of the pudding basin with parchment paper or aluminum foil and a pudding cloth. Tie the pudding cloth securely with string and gather any excess pudding cloth over the top of the basin.

   Note: The pudding cloth is optional, however, you need to make sure that no water gets into the basin while it's steaming. I like to use a pudding cloth because that's the way I've always done it. And, it makes it easier to get the pudding into and out of the pot.

9. Place the trivet in the stainless steel liner of the Instant Pot.

10. Add approximately 6 cups (1.4 L) of boiling water to the inner pot (This worked perfect for the basin I used in a 6-quart Instant Pot. The goal is to have the water be about 1" (2.5 cm) below the rim of the pudding basin. Adjust the amount of boiling water to suit your pot and basin.)

11. Gently lower the prepared pudding basin onto the trivet.

12. Check the water level in relation to the pudding basin and adjust if necessary.

13. Close and lock the lid of the Instant Pot, ensuring the Pressure Valve is in the Sealing position.

14. Select the Steam function and set the cooking time for 45 minutes.

15. Once cooking time is complete allow for a complete Natural Pressure Release (Wait for the float valve to drop on its own. This can take up to 45 minutes.)

16. Remove the completed pudding from the Instant Pot and carefully remove the pudding cloth and parchment paper or aluminum foil.

17. Allow the pudding to cool for 10-15 minutes.

18. You can turn the pudding out at this point and allow it to continue cooling while you start the next one in your Instant Pot.

Tip: If you have more than one basin, you can be preparing the next one while the previous one is cooking.

Serve with a brandy or rum sauce which you can light just before bringing to the table. The flame may be difficult to see unless you turn out the lights.

Tip: The pudding can be reheated by steaming for about 8 to 10 minutes in the Instant Pot. Follow the directions given above and reduce the cooking time to 10 minutes.

Tip: These puddings will freeze well. Wrap in two layers of waxed paper and then in aluminum foil. Allow to thaw at room temperature when you remove them from the freezer.

FIGGY PUDDING

INGREDIENTS

¾ cup (95g) <u>suet</u> (<u>see page 140 for alternatives</u>)

¾ cup (135g) brown sugar, packed

3 eggs

¼ cup (60 mL) cream sherry

1 cup (150g) figs, chopped

¼ cup (60 mL) molasses

1 teaspoon (5 mL) ground cinnamon

1½ cups (135g) dried bread crumbs

1 teaspoon (5 mL) vanilla

METHOD

1. Generously grease a 2 pint (950 mL) pudding basin and then coat with white sugar.

2. In a large bowl, combine the suet and brown sugar and mix well.

3. Add the eggs, vanilla and molasses and beat until well mixed.

4. Add the dried bread crumbs and cinnamon and mix until combined.

5. Add the cream sherry and mix just enough to make sure the sherry is well incorporated into the mixture.

6. Fold in the chopped figs.

   Note: If you are using dried figs, rehydrate them by putting them in a small saucepan covered with water. Bring them to a boil, reduce heat and allow them to simmer for about 15 minutes. Pour off the excess liquid, allow the figs to cool and then coarsely chop them.

7. Pour the completed batter into the prepared pudding basin.

8. Cover the top of the pudding basin with parchment paper or aluminum foil and a pudding cloth. Tie the pudding

cloth securely with string and gather any excess pudding cloth over the top of the basin.

Note: The pudding cloth is optional, however, you need to make sure that no water gets into the basin while it's steaming. I like to use a pudding cloth because that's the way I've always done it. And, it makes it easier to get the pudding into and out of the pot.

9. Place the trivet in the stainless steel liner of the Instant Pot.

10. Add approximately 6 cups (1.4 L) of boiling water to the inner pot (This worked perfect for the basin I used in a 6-quart Instant Pot. The goal is to have the water be about 1" (2.5 cm) below the rim of the pudding basin. Adjust the amount of boiling water to suit your pot and basin.)

11. Gently lower the prepared pudding basin onto the trivet. Check the water level in relation to the pudding basin and adjust if necessary.

12. Close and lock the lid of the Instant Pot, ensuring the Pressure Valve is in the Sealing position.

13. Select the Steam function and set the cooking time for 90 minutes.

14. Once cooking time is complete allow for a complete Natural Pressure Release (Wait for the float valve to drop on its own. This can take up to 45 minutes.)

15. Remove the completed pudding from the Instant Pot and carefully remove the pudding cloth and parchment paper or aluminum foil.

16. Allow the pudding to cool for 10-15 minutes.

17. Invert on a serving dish, if desired.

18. Serve with Bird's custard, heavy cream or ice cream.

Ginger Pudding

Ingredients

1 cup (120g) all purpose flour
1½ teaspoons (7.5 mL) ground ginger
¼ teaspoon (1.25 mL) baking soda
½ cup (120 mL) milk
2 tablespoons (30 mL) Tate & Lyle's Golden Syrup
2 tablespoons (30 mL) preserved ginger, chopped
1 egg
1½ cups (135g) bread crumbs
1 tablespoon (15 mL) brown sugar
1½ cups (190g) suet (see page 140 for alternatives)

Method

1. In a small bowl, combine the flour, ground ginger and baking soda. Mix well and set aside.

2. In a small saucepan, heat the milk just to the simmering point, remove from heat and add the golden syrup and the beaten egg. Mix well.

   Note: golden corn syrup may be substituted if you cannot get Tate & Lyle's Golden Syrup

3. Stir in the bread crumbs, sugar, suet and chopped, preserved ginger. Add the flour mixture and stir to combine everything well.

4. Pour the completed mixture into a well greased 2 pint (950 mL) pudding basin.

5. Cover the top of the pudding basin with parchment paper or aluminum foil and a pudding cloth. Tie the pudding cloth securely with string and gather any excess pudding cloth over the top of the basin.

   Note: The pudding cloth is optional, however, you need to make sure that no water gets into the basin while it's steaming. I like to use a pudding cloth because that's the way I've always done it. And, it makes it easier to get the pudding into and out of the pot.

155

6. Place the trivet in the stainless steel liner of the Instant Pot.

7. Add approximately 6 cups (1.4 L) of boiling water to the inner pot (This worked perfect for the basin I used in a 6-quart Instant Pot. The goal is to have the water be about 1" (2.5 cm) below the rim of the pudding basin. Adjust the amount of boiling water to suit your pot and basin.)

8. Gently lower the prepared pudding basin onto the trivet. Check the water level in relation to the pudding basin and adjust if necessary.

9. Close and lock the lid of the Instant Pot, ensuring the Pressure Valve is in the Sealing position.

10. Select the Steam function and set the cooking time for 60 minutes.

11. Once cooking time is complete allow for a complete Natural Pressure Release (Wait for the float valve to drop on its own. This can take up to 45 minutes or more.)

12. Remove the completed pudding from the Instant Pot and carefully remove the pudding cloth and parchment paper or aluminum foil.

13. Allow the pudding to cool for 10-15 minutes.

14. Invert on a serving dish, if desired.

15. Serve with Bird's custard, heavy cream or ice cream.

JAM ROLY-POLY

INGREDIENTS

1 recipe <u>sweet suet pastry</u> (see page 143)
5 - 6 tablespoons (75 - 90 mL) jam of your choice

METHOD

1. On a lightly floured surface, roll out the suet pastry to create a rectangle approximately 6½ to 7 inches (16.5 to 17.5 cm) by 10 to 11 inches (25 to 28 cm). (It needs to be sized to fit into the inner liner of your Instant Pot.)

2. Spread the rolled dough with the jam of your choice. The traditional choices are often raspberry or strawberry jam.

3. Spread the jam to about ½ an inch (1.25 cm) away from the edges.

4. Use some cold water to slightly wet the edges of the pastry. Then, roll up the pastry, from the shorter edge and seal the edges and seam.

5. Wrap the roly-poly well in 2 or 3 layers of aluminum foil and twist the ends to seal.

6. Place the trivet in the inner liner and pour in 2 cups (480 mL) of boiling water.

7. Carefully place the foil-wrapped pudding on the trivet.

8. Close and lock the lid of the Instant Pot, ensuring the Pressure Valve is in the Sealing position.

9. Select the Steam function and set the cooking time for 45 minutes.

10. Once cooking time is complete allow for a complete Natural Pressure Release (Wait for the float valve to drop on its own. This can take up to 45 minutes.)

11. Remove the completed Roly-Poly from the Instant Pot and allow to cool on a wire rack for 5-10 minutes.

12. Carefully remove the aluminum foil and slice into serving portions.

13. Serve with Bird's custard, heavy cream or ice cream.

LEICESTERSHIRE PUDDING

INGREDIENTS

1½ cups (225g) raisins, seedless
1 cup (120g) all purpose flour
¾ cup (95g) <u>suet</u>, chopped (<u>see page 140 for alternatives</u>)
2 eggs, beaten
1 teaspoon (5 mL) grated lemon peel
1 teaspoon (5 mL) nutmeg, freshly grated
2 tablespoons (30 mL) brandy
milk

METHOD

1. Grease a 1½ pint (700 mL) pudding basin.

2. In a large bowl, combine the raisins, flour and suet and mix well.

3. Add the beaten eggs, lemon peel, nutmeg and brandy. Mix well.

4. Knead in enough milk to produce a firm dough and transfer the mixture into the greased pudding basin.

5. Cover the top of the pudding basin with parchment paper or aluminum foil and a pudding cloth. Tie the pudding cloth securely with string and gather any excess pudding cloth over the top of the basin.

   Note: The pudding cloth is optional, however, you need to make sure that no water gets into the basin while it's steaming. I like to use a pudding cloth because that's the way I've always done it. And, it makes it easier to get the pudding into and out of the pot.

6. Place the trivet in the stainless steel liner of the Instant Pot.

7. Add approximately 6 cups (1.4 L) of boiling water to the inner pot (This worked perfect for the basin I used in a 6-quart Instant Pot. The goal is to have the water be about 1" (2.5 cm) below the rim of the pudding basin. Adjust the amount of boiling water to suit your pot and basin.)

8. Gently lower the prepared pudding basin onto the trivet. Check the water level in relation to the pudding basin and adjust if necessary.

9. Close and lock the lid of the Instant Pot, ensuring the Pressure Valve is in the Sealing position.

10. Select the Steam function and set the cooking time for 120 minutes.

11. Once cooking time is complete allow for a complete Natural Pressure Release (Wait for the float valve to drop on its own. This can take up to 45 minutes.)

12. Remove the completed pudding from the Instant Pot and carefully remove the pudding cloth and parchment paper or aluminum foil.

13. Allow the pudding to cool for 10-15 minutes.

14. Invert on a serving dish, if desired.

15. Serve with Bird's custard, heavy cream or ice cream.

LEMONY SUSSEX POND PUDDING

INGREDIENTS FOR PUDDING

   1 recipe <u>sweet suet pastry</u> (see page 143)
   zest of 1 lemon
   ½ cup (45g) breadcrumbs

INGREDIENTS FOR FILLING

   ¾ cup (170g) cold butter, cut into small cubes
   ¾ cup (135g) brown sugar
   1 large whole lemon, (this is a 2nd lemon with the skin intact)

METHOD

1. When making the sweet suet pastry for this recipe, add the zest of one lemon and the breadcrumbs.

2. Grease a 1½ quart (1.5 L) pudding basin.

3. Roll out the sweet suet pastry and line the pudding basin with the pastry. Reserve enough pastry to make a lid for after you have filled the pudding.

4. Put the lemon on a hard surface and roll it with your hand several times. This will help to release the juice. Prick the lemon all over with a fork or toothpick.

5. Add half the sugar, butter to the pastry-lined basin and place the whole lemon on top.

6. Place the remaining sugar and butter around the edge of the lemon.

7. Wet the edges of the suet pastry lid and place on top. Pinch the edges to seal.

8. Cover the top of the pudding basin with parchment paper or aluminum foil and a pudding cloth. Tie the pudding cloth securely with string and gather any excess pudding cloth over the top of the basin.

   Note: The pudding cloth is optional, however, you need to make sure that no water gets into the basin while it's steaming. I like to use a pudding cloth because that's the way I've always done it. And, it makes it easier to get the pudding into and out of the pot.

9. Place the trivet in the stainless steel liner of the Instant Pot.

10. Add approximately 6 cups (1.4 L) of boiling water to the inner pot (This worked perfect for the basin I used in a 6-quart Instant Pot. The goal is to have the water be about 1" (2.5 cm) below the rim of the pudding basin. Adjust the amount of boiling water to suit your pot and basin.)

11. Gently lower the prepared pudding basin onto the trivet. Check the water level in relation to the pudding basin and adjust if necessary.

12. Close and lock the lid of the Instant Pot, ensuring the Pressure Valve is in the Sealing position.

13. Select the Steam function and set the cooking time for 90 minutes.

14. Once cooking time is complete allow for a complete Natural Pressure Release (Wait for the float valve to drop on its own. This can take up to 45 minutes.)

15. Remove the completed pudding from the Instant Pot and carefully remove the pudding cloth and parchment paper or aluminum foil.

16. Allow the pudding to cool for 10-15 minutes.

17. Invert on a serving dish, if desired.

18. Serve with Bird's custard, heavy cream or ice cream.

Middlesex Pond Pudding

You will notice that this is very similar to the previous recipe for the Sussex Pond Pudding. Middlesex is the county I was born in so, as this was my variation, I named it thus but this is the only place you will find anything called a Middlesex Pond Pudding.

Ingredients

1 recipe sweet suet pastry (see page 143)
zest of ½ orange
½ cup (45g) breadcrumbs

Filling

1 small lemon, thinly sliced
1 small lime, thinly sliced
1 small orange, thinly sliced
2 tablespoons (15g) all purpose flour
¾ cup (135g) brown sugar
½ cup (120g) cold butter, cut into small cubes

Method

1. Grease a 1½ pint (700 mL) pudding basin.

2. When making the sweet suet pastry for this recipe, add the orange zest and the breadcrumbs.

3. Roll out the sweet suet pastry and line the pudding basin with the pastry. Reserve enough pastry to make a lid for after you have filled the pudding.

4. In a medium bowl toss the lemon, lime and orange slices with the 2 tablespoons (15g) of all purpose flour.

5. To make the filling, create layers starting with 2 tablespoons (25g) of the brown sugar, 3 or 4 cubes of butter and a few slices of lemon, lime and orange. Continue with these layers until you've used up all of the filling ingredients.

6. Wet the edges of the suet pastry lid and place on top. Pinch the edges to seal.

7. Cover the top of the pudding basin with parchment paper or aluminum foil and a pudding cloth. Tie the pudding cloth securely with string and gather any excess pudding cloth over the top of the basin.

   Note: The pudding cloth is optional, however, you need to make sure that no water gets into the basin while it's steaming. I like to use a pudding cloth because that's the way I've always done it. And, it makes it easier to get the pudding into and out of the pot.

8. Place the trivet in the stainless steel liner of the Instant Pot.

9. Add approximately 6 cups (1.4 L) of boiling water to the inner pot (This worked perfect for the basin I used in a 6-quart Instant Pot. The goal is to have the water be about 1" (2.5 cm) below the rim of the pudding basin. Adjust the amount of boiling water to suit your pot and basin.)

10. Gently lower the prepared pudding basin onto the trivet. Check the water level in relation to the pudding basin and adjust if necessary.

11. Close and lock the lid of the Instant Pot, ensuring the Pressure Valve is in the Sealing position.

12. Select the Steam function and set the cooking time for 90 minutes.

13. Once cooking time is complete allow for a complete Natural Pressure Release (Wait for the float valve to drop on its own. This can take up to 45 minutes.)

14. Remove the completed pudding from the Instant Pot and carefully remove the pudding cloth and parchment paper or aluminum foil.

15. Allow the pudding to cool for 10-15 minutes.

16. Invert on a serving dish, if desired.

17. Serve with Bird's custard, heavy cream or ice cream.

Treacle Pudding

Ingredients

¼ cup (60 mL) dark treacle, substitute molasses if you can't find treacle

¼ cup (60 mL) Tate & Lyle's golden syrup, substitute corn syrup if you can't find Tate & Lyle's

¼ teaspoon (1.25 mL) cinnamon

2 cups (240g) all purpose flour

3 teaspoons (15 mL) baking powder

1 cup (125g) suet, finely chopped (see page 140 for alternatives)

⅓ cup (60g) brown sugar

⅓ cup (65g) white sugar

⅔ cup (160 mL) milk

2 eggs, beaten

Method

1. Grease a 1½ pint (700 mL) pudding basin.

   Note: make sure to grease the basin well or the treacle might stick.

2. Pour the treacle and golden syrup into the base of the pudding basin.

3. In a medium bowl combine the flour, cinnamon and baking powder and mix well. Cut in the suet with a pastry blender until the mixture resembles a coarse meal.

4. Add both the white and brown sugar to the flour mixture and stir well.

5. In a medium bowl, combine the milk and beaten eggs.

6. Slowly pour the egg mixture into the flour mixture and stir until all ingredients are well combined and make a soft, sticky dough.

7. Carefully spoon the dough into the pudding basin being careful not to disturb the treacle too much.

8. Cover the top of the pudding basin with parchment paper or aluminum foil and a pudding cloth. Tie the pudding cloth securely with string and gather any excess pudding cloth over the top of the basin.

Note: The pudding cloth is optional, however, you need to make sure that no water gets into the basin while it's steaming. I like to use a pudding cloth because that's the way I've always done it. And, it makes it easier to get the pudding into and out of the pot.

9. Place the trivet in the stainless steel liner of the Instant Pot.

10. Add approximately 6 cups (1.4 L) of boiling water to the inner pot (This worked perfect for the basin I used in a 6-quart Instant Pot. The goal is to have the water be about 1" (2.5 cm) below the rim of the pudding basin. Adjust the amount of boiling water to suit your pot and basin.)

11. Gently lower the prepared pudding basin onto the trivet. Check the water level in relation to the pudding basin and adjust if necessary.

12. Close and lock the lid of the Instant Pot, ensuring the Pressure Valve is in the Sealing position.

13. Select the Steam function and set the cooking time for 60 minutes.

14. Once cooking time is complete allow for a complete Natural Pressure Release (Wait for the float valve to drop on its own. This can take up to 45 minutes.)

15. Remove the completed pudding from the Instant Pot and carefully remove the pudding cloth and parchment paper or aluminum foil.

16. Allow the pudding to cool on a wire rack for 5 minutes and then invert the pudding on a serving plate, allowing the treacle to dribble down the sides.

Simple Jam Steamed Pudding

This steamed pudding is much like making a cake but it's steamed in the Instant Pot instead of being baked in a regular oven.

Ingredients

1⅓ cups (160g) all-purpose flour
1½ teaspoons (7.5 mL) baking powder
¼ teaspoon (1.25 mL) salt
½ cup (120g) butter, softened
⅓ cup (65g) white granulated sugar
2 large eggs
1 teaspoon (5 mL) vanilla
½ cup (120 mL) milk
⅓ cup (80 mL) strawberry jam (see recipe for homemade Instant Pot Strawberry Jam on page 11)

Method

1. In a small bowl, combine the flour, baking powder and salt. Mix well and set aside.

2. In a medium bowl beat together the butter and sugar, using an electric mixer on low, until pale and creamy.

3. Add the eggs one at a time, beating well after each addition.

4. Stir in the vanilla.

5. Add about half of the flour mixture and mix well, then add half of the milk and mix. Repeat with the rest of the flour mixture and milk. Mix until just combined.

6. Grease a 1½ pint (700 mL) pudding basin.

   Note: make sure to grease the basin well or the strawberry jam might stick.

7. Put the strawberry jam in the bottom of the pudding basin.

8. Carefully pour the dough into the pudding basin being careful not to disturb the jam too much.

9. Cover the top of the pudding basin with parchment paper or aluminum foil and a pudding cloth. Tie the pudding cloth securely with string and gather any excess pudding cloth over the top of the basin.

   Note: The pudding cloth is optional, however, you need to make sure that no water gets into the basin while it's steaming. I like to use a pudding cloth because that's the way I've always done it. And, it makes it easier to get the pudding into and out of the pot.

10. Place the trivet in the stainless steel liner of the Instant Pot.

11. Add approximately 6 cups (1.4 L) of boiling water to the inner pot (This worked perfect for the basin I used in a 6-quart Instant Pot. The goal is to have the water be about 1" (2.5 cm) below the rim of the pudding basin. Adjust the amount of boiling water to suit your pot and basin.)

12. Gently lower the prepared pudding basin onto the trivet. Check the water level in relation to the pudding basin and adjust if necessary.

13. Close and lock the lid of the Instant Pot, ensuring the Pressure Valve is in the Sealing position.

14. Select the Steam function and set the cooking time for 60 minutes.

15. Once cooking time is complete allow for a complete Natural Pressure Release (Wait for the float valve to drop on its own. This can take up to 45 minutes.)

16. Remove the completed pudding from the Instant Pot and carefully remove the pudding cloth and parchment paper or aluminum foil.

17. Allow the pudding to cool on a wire rack for 5 minutes and then invert the pudding on a serving plate, allowing the jam to dribble down the sides.

CHEESE AND LEEK SUET PUDDING

INGREDIENTS

1 recipe savoury suet pastry (see page 142)

Filling

3 tablespoons (40g) butter
1 pound (450g) leeks
2 tablespoons (15g) all purpose flour
1 cup (100g) sharp cheddar cheese, shredded
¼ cup (60 mL) water
1 teaspoon (5 mL) dried thyme
sea salt, to taste
freshly ground black pepper, to taste

METHOD

1. Cut the leeks in half, lengthwise and clean well. Remove the tougher green pieces and slice the white and light green portions only..

2. In a large skillet, melt the butter over low heat and add the leeks. Cook for about 10 minutes or until soft. Sprinkle the flour over the leeks, mix well and continue to cook, over low heat, for another 2 minutes.

3. Slowly add the milk, stirring constantly. Then add the grated cheese and stir well to combine.

4. When the mixture begins to thicken, remove from heat and stir in the salt and pepper to taste. Set aside and allow the mixture to cool completely.

5. Once the cheese and leek filling has cooled, grease a 2 pint (950 mL) pudding basin, roll out the suet pastry and line the pudding basin with the pastry. Ladle the filling into the basin and then cover with a pastry lid.

6. Cover the top of the pudding basin with parchment paper or aluminum foil and a pudding cloth. Tie the pudding cloth securely with string and gather any excess pudding cloth over the top of the basin.

Note: The pudding cloth is optional, however, you need to make sure that no water gets into the basin while it's steaming. I like to use a pudding cloth because that's the way I've always done it. And, it makes it easier to get the pudding into and out of the pot.

7. Place the trivet in the stainless steel liner of the Instant Pot.

8. Add approximately 6 cups (1.4 L) of boiling water to the inner pot (This worked perfect for the basin I used in a 6-quart Instant Pot. The goal is to have the water be about 1" (2.5 cm) below the rim of the pudding basin. Adjust the amount of boiling water to suit your pot and basin.)

9. Gently lower the prepared pudding basin onto the trivet. Check the water level in relation to the pudding basin and adjust if necessary.

10. Close and lock the lid of the Instant Pot, ensuring the Pressure Valve is in the Sealing position.

11. Select the Steam function and set the cooking time for 120 minutes.

12. Once cooking time is complete allow for a complete Natural Pressure Release (Wait for the float valve to drop on its own. This can take up to 45 minutes.)

13. Remove the completed pudding from the Instant Pot and carefully remove the pudding cloth and parchment paper or aluminum foil.

14. Allow the pudding to cool on a wire rack for 5-10 minutes and serve.

Ham and Leek Suet Pudding

Ingredients

1 recipe savoury <u>suet</u> pastry (see page 142)

Filling

12 ounces (340g) cooked ham
1 leek
1½ tablespoons (25g) butter
1½ tablespoons (11g) all purpose flour
1 cup (240 mL) chicken stock
2 sprigs fresh thyme
pepper, to taste

Method

1. Cut the cooked ham into small cubes. Wash the leek well and remove the tough green top of the leek. Then cut the leek into thin slices.

2. In a medium saucepan, melt the butter over medium heat and cook the leek slices until tender. Sprinkle the flour over the leeks and stir well.

3. Slowly add the hot chicken stock, stirring constantly. Continue stirring, over medium heat, until the mixture comes to a boil and begins to thicken.

4. Reduce heat and add the thyme, cream and ham.

5. Stir well and simmer for about 5 minutes.

6. Remove from heat and set aside to cool.

7. Once the ham and leek filling has cooled, grease a 2 pint (950 mL) pudding basin, roll out the suet pastry and line the pudding basin with the pastry. Ladle the filling into the basin and then cover with a pastry lid.

8. Cover the top of the pudding basin with parchment paper or aluminum foil and a pudding cloth. Tie the pudding cloth securely with string and gather any excess pudding cloth over the top of the basin.

Note: The pudding cloth is optional, however, you need to make sure that no water gets into the basin while it's steaming. I like to use a pudding cloth because that's the way I've always done it. And, it makes it easier to get the pudding into and out of the pot.

9. Place the trivet in the stainless steel liner of the Instant Pot.

10. Add approximately 6 cups (1.4 L) of boiling water to the inner pot (This worked perfect for the basin I used in a 6-quart Instant Pot. The goal is to have the water be about 1" (2.5 cm) below the rim of the pudding basin. Adjust the amount of boiling water to suit your pot and basin.)

11. Gently lower the prepared pudding basin onto the trivet. Check the water level in relation to the pudding basin and adjust if necessary.

12. Close and lock the lid of the Instant Pot, ensuring the Pressure Valve is in the Sealing position.

13. Select the Steam function and set the cooking time for 60 minutes.

14. Once cooking time is complete allow for a complete Natural Pressure Release (Wait for the float valve to drop on its own. This can take up to 45 minutes.)

15. Remove the completed pudding from the Instant Pot and carefully remove the pudding cloth and parchment paper or aluminum foil.

16. Allow the pudding to cool for 10-15 minutes.

17. Invert on a serving dish, if desired.

Steak and Kidney Pudding

Making The Filling

The filling of a steak and kidney pudding is actually a steak and kidney stew. The Instant Pot excels at stew and with this recipe you will be sure to make the best beef stew you have ever tasted (see the recipe on page 36). Save what won't fit in your pudding basin to add to the pudding as you serve or freeze it and serve another day as stew.

Pudding Ingredients

> 1 recipe savoury suet pastry (see page 142)
> 3 - 4 cups (700 - 900 mL) of the Steak & Kidney stew.
> ¼ cup (60 mL) of the gravy from the stew

Method

1. Grease a 2 pint (950 mL) pudding basin.

2. Roll out the suet pastry, using ¾ of the pastry for the lining and ¼ for lid.

3. Line the pudding basin with the pastry and gently ladle the filling into the basin.

   Use a slotted spoon to avoid putting too much liquid in the pudding which will make the pastry mushy.

   Make sure the filling is cold or at least cool.

4. The basin should be almost full with the drained filling.

5. Add ¼ cup (60 mL) of the reserved gravy to the filling.

6. Carefully add the pastry lid and pinch all around the edge to seal it.

7. Cover the top of the pudding with parchment paper or aluminum foil and a pudding cloth.

8. Tie the pudding cloth securely with string and gather any excess pudding cloth over the top of the basin.

   Note: The pudding cloth is optional, however, you need to make sure that no water gets into the basin while it's steaming. I like to use a pudding cloth because that's the way I've always done it. And, it makes it easier to get the pudding into and out of the pot.

9. Place the trivet in the stainless steel liner of the Instant Pot.

10. Add approximately 6 cups (1.4 L) of boiling water to the inner pot (This worked for the basin I used in a 6 quart (6 litre)Instant Pot.

    The goal is to have the water be about 1"(2.5 cm) below the rim of the pudding basin. Adjust the amount of boiling water to suit your pot and basin.

11. Gently lower the prepared pudding basin onto the trivet. Check the water level in relation to the pudding basin and adjust if necessary.

12. Close and lock the lid of the Instant Pot, ensuring the Pressure Valve is in the Sealing position.

13. Select the Steam function and set the cooking time for 45 minutes.

14. Once cooking time is complete allow for a complete Natural Pressure Release (Wait for the float valve to drop on its own. This can take up to 45 minutes.)

15. Remove the completed pudding from the Instant Pot and carefully remove the pudding cloth and parchment paper or aluminum foil.

16. Allow the pudding to cool for 5 - 10 minutes.

    Note: This pudding should be served directly from the basin, not turned out onto a plate.

17. Serve the pudding with the rest of the gravy (reheated separately), boiled potatoes and fresh peas or scarlet runner beans.

DESSERTS

This section looks a little light but that's because I decided to put all the steamed desserts in the steamed pudding section.

I think you will enjoy the few that are left and remember you can make any dessert Authentic English by covering it in Bird's Custard, (If you're a Brit you know what I mean).

If you're looking for a book full of British dessert ideas check out volume 2 in this series *How To Make Sherry Trifle A Traditional Dessert*

https://ebooks.geezerguides.com/how-to-make-sherry-trifle-and-british-fools-traditional-english-deserts/

You might also enjoy volume 9, *How To Bake British Cakes, Crumpets, Buns & Biscuits.*

https://ebooks.geezerguides.com/how-to-bake-british-cakes-crumpets-buns-biscuits/

BANOFFEE PIE

We Brits love our sweets and this pie is amazing! But, trust me, you'll want to limit it to special occasions because of the calories.

This is a very simple recipe for a really impressive result. Serve it to friends because the fatter they get, the better you will look.

INGREDIENTS

For the Crust
2 cups (200g) Digestive biscuits, crushed (approximately 12 biscuits)
⅓ cup (80g) butter

For the Filling
1 recipe of Instant Pot Dulce de Leche (see recipe on page 179)
3 small ripe bananas
1¼ cups (300 mL) Greek yogurt or sour cream (or a combination of the two as long as the total measurement remains the same)
½ teaspoon (2.5 mL) vanilla extract

FOR THE GARNISH

Melted Toffee or Caramel sauce (optional)

METHOD

Making the Pie Crust
Tip: You can do this step while the milk is cooking.

1. Crush the Digestive biscuits well and add to a medium bowl.

2. Melt the butter, pour over the crushed biscuits and mix well.

3. Press the mixture into a 9-inch (23 cm) pie plate, distributing evenly and up the sides as well.

4. Refrigerate well, until needed.

Putting the Pie Together

1. Once the dulce de leche is completely cooled to room temperature, pour it into a medium bowl.

2. Cut the bananas into thin slices and fold into the dulce de leche.

3. Remove the crust from the fridge and pour the banana mixture into the crust.

4. In another bowl, combine the yogurt (or sour cream) with the vanilla and mix well.

5. Smooth the yogurt (or sour cream) mixture over the banana mixture.

6. Drizzle with melted toffee or caramel sauce, if using.

7. Serve immediately or refrigerate, lightly covered with plastic wrap, for later use.

SERVINGS: 8 SLICES

INSTANT POT DULCE DE LECHE

According to Wikipedia, dulce de leche is a confection prepared by slowly heating sweetened milk to create a substance that derives its flavor from the Maillard reaction, also changing color, with an appearance and flavor similar to caramel. Literally translated, it means "jam [made] of milk" or "sweet [made] of milk."

There are several methods out there for making dulce de leche in the Instant Pot but I've found this to be the easiest and safest way.

This sweet, caramel-flavored treat can also be used as a cake (or cheesecake) topping, a spread between two cookies, a sweetener in your coffee and more.

Warning: Several of the methods you might find online suggest you put an unopened can in your Instant Pot. Although this might work I think it is a little risky particularly with the type of cans with a pull tab. This type of can is scored so that it will open easily and just does not have the structural integrity to withstand the pressure inside your Instant Pot.

INGREDIENTS

>   1 - 14 ounce (397g) can sweetened condensed milk
>   Water (see Method)

METHOD

1. Remove the labels from the can of sweetened condensed milk and then remove the lid. (Yes, open the can.)

2. Cover the entire, open, can tightly with aluminum foil.

3. Place the can on a trivet in the Instant Pot and add enough water to come halfway up the can.

4. Close and lock the lid ensuring the Pressure Valve is in the Sealing position.

5. Select Manual/Pressure Cook mode and set the cooking time for 30 minutes.

6. When the cooking time is complete allow a full Natural Pressure Release which will take more than an hour.

7. Once the pressure is completely released and the Float Valve has dropped, carefully remove the lid.

8. Carefully remove the can from the pot and transfer to a wire rack to cool.

9. Carefully remove, or just open, the foil to allow it to cool more quickly.

Egg Custard

Egg custard for dessert was always a regular occurrence in our house when I was a kid. To this day, it remains one of my favorites. Now, with the Instant Pot, it is even easier to make.

Ingredients

> 4 cups (950 mL) whole milk
> 6 large eggs
> ¾ cup (150g) white granulated sugar
> 1 teaspoon (5 mL) vanilla extract
> Nutmeg, freshly grated

Method

1. In a medium bowl, beat the eggs.
2. Add the milk, sugar and vanilla and blend until combined.
3. Divide the mixture equally between six oven-safe ceramic custard cups/ramekins.
4. Grate a little nutmeg on top of each custard cup.
5. Add 1½ cups (350 mL) of water to inner liner of the Instant Pot and place the trivet in bottom.
6. Carefully place the custard cups on the trivet.

   Note: you'll need to stack the custard cups, so you'll need a second trivet to place on top of the first 3 custard cups.

7. Cover the first 3 custard cups lightly with aluminum foil, and poke a few small holes in the foil.
8. Place the second trivet, arrange the next 3 custard cups and cover them loosely with foil, as well, poking few small holes in that layer, too
9. Close and lock the lid ensuring the Pressure Valve is in the Sealing position.
10. Select Manual/Pressure Cook mode and set the cooking time for 2 minutes. (Push the "+" or "-" buttons to set the required cooking time.)

Tip: If you are using glass custard cups, increase cooking time to 4 minutes.

11. Once cooking time is complete, allow a 10 minute Natural Pressure Release and then release the rest of the pressure by carefully turning the Pressure Valve from Sealing to Venting.

12. Once all of the pressure has been released and the Float Valve has dropped, carefully remove the lid.

13. Remove the custards from the Instant Pot and allow to cool on a wire rack.

14. The custards can be served warm or refrigerated and served cold later.

Individual Almond Apple Bread Puddings

I was going to call this one Toasted Almond Apple Cinnamon Raisin Bread Pudding, but the title just seemed way too long. There's lots of good stuff going on in here; chopped toasted almonds, chopped apple, cinnamon raisin bread (homemade or store bought) and a bonus Dark Rum Sauce recipe to boot!

Marry all of this with the fact that the bread pudding can be made in the Instant Pot and you've got an amazing dessert that everyone will love!

Ingredients

4 cups (950 mL) cinnamon raisin bread (homemade or store bought), torn into small chunks
3 large eggs
½ cup (100g) brown sugar, packed
¼ cup (55g) butter, melted
2 teaspoons (10 mL) vanilla
1 teaspoon (5 mL) cinnamon
¼ teaspoon (1.25 mL) allspice
¼ teaspoon (1.25 mL) salt
2 cups (475 mL) whole milk
1 apple, cored and chopped
½ cup (70g) chopped toasted almonds*

Method

1. Tear enough bread into approximately ½ inch (1.25 cm) pieces to measure 4 cups (950 mL) and place in a large bowl.

2. In a medium bowl beat the eggs with a fork. Add the sugar, melted butter, vanilla and spices and stir until sugar is dissolved.

3. Add the milk and mix well.

4. Add the egg and milk mixture to the bread and mix well.

5. Allow the bread/egg/milk mixture to sit for 5 minutes and mix well once more, mashing slightly to break up some of the pieces of bread.

6. Fold in the chopped apple and chopped toasted almonds.

7. Pour about ⅔ cup (160 mL) each into six greased ramekins.

8. Pour 1½ cups (350 mL) of water in the inner pot of your instant pot and place a trivet on top.

   Note: Depending on the size of your ramekins, you may have to do two tiers if you have the appropriate trivets. If not, you can make these in two batches, or make the bread pudding in a single, larger dish (increase cooking time to 18 minutes if you use one large dish).

   Important Note: Always be sure that the ramekins or dishes you choose are safe to use in your Instant Pot

9. Place the bread pudding(s) in your Instant Pot on top of the trivet(s) and cover lightly with foil or a silicon lid.

10. Close and lock the lid, ensuring that the pressure valve is in the Sealing position.

11. Select the Manual/Pressure Cook mode and set the cooking time for 10 minutes.

12. Once the cooking time is complete, allow a 10 minute Natural Pressure Release then manually release the rest of the pressure.

13. Once the pressure has been released, and the Float Valve has dropped, carefully unlock and remove the lid.

14. Transfer the bread pudding(s) to a wire rack to cool slightly.

    Note: You can also allow them to cool completely and refrigerate or freeze and then reheat later.

15. Serve with Dark Rum Sauce (bonus recipe below) or with a topping of your choice.

*To toast the almonds, coarsely chopped and spread them on a small baking sheet in a single layer. Toast in a 350°F (175°C, Gas Mark 4) oven for 3-4 minutes, shake and stir and then bake for another 2-3 minutes. Remove from oven and allow to cool.

Dark Rum Sauce
for Bread Pudding

For an extra special treat to give your bread pudding a kick.

Ingredients

¼ cup (55g) butter

1 large egg

½ teaspoon (2.5 mL) vanilla

½ cup (100g) brown sugar, packed

½ cup (120 mL) dark rum

Method

1. In a small saucepan, over medium-low heat, melt the butter.

2. Add the egg and vanilla and whisk until smooth.

3. Add the sugar and whisk all ingredients together.

4. Bring to a simmer, whisking the mixture continuously until thick and creamy.

5. Add the dark rum while continuing to whisk.

6. If the mixture is too thin, reduce it by allowing it to simmer, whisking frequently, until you get the right consistency.

APPENDIX

That's it you've come to the end - now go back and make something.

When you have made a few of the recipes please go back to where you purchased and leave a review. There are millions of books available and the most important asset an independent author can have is reviews from satisfied readers.

In the next couple of pages you will learn how you can get a free membership to our Instant Pot video site and also how you can get another one of our books (your choice) absolutely free.

And please don't forget to leave a review!

Thank you,

Geoff Wells

INSTANT POT RECIPES

The Instant Pot has now found an important place in my and Vicky's kitchen. We use it every day and have converted many of our favorite recipes to work in the Instant Pot.

We use this new appliance so much we decided to add this new volume to the Authentic English Recipes series with just Instant Pot directions for lots of our favorite British recipes.

We are also adding videos for all these recipes to our

https://instantpotvideorecipes.com

membership site.

As one of our loyal readers you get a free membership to this site as a bonus for buying this book. All you do is visit the secret claim page to get your 100% discount coupon code.

https://fun.geezerguides.com/freemembership

BONUS ~ CLAIM YOUR FREE BOOK

Thank you for buying this book! As a bonus we would like to give you another one absolutely free - No Strings Attached

You can choose any of the books in our catalog as your bonus. Just use this link or scan the QR code below -

https://fun.geezerguides.com/freebook

Please Review

As independent publishers, we rely on reviews and word-of-mouth recommendations to get the word out about our books.

If you've enjoyed this book, please consider leaving a review at the website you purchased it from.

If You're Not Satisfied

We aspire to the highest standards with all our books. If, for some reason, you're not satisfied, please let us know and we will try to make it right. You can always return the book for a full refund but we hope you will reserve that as a last option.

About The Author

Geoff Wells was born in a small town outside London, England just after the 2nd World War. He left home at sixteen and emigrated to Canada, settling in the Toronto area of Southern Ontario. He had many jobs and interests early in life from real estate sales to helicopter pilot to restaurant owner. When the personal computer era began he finally settled down and became a computer programmer until he took early retirement. Now, as an author, he has written several popular series including: Authentic English Recipes, Reluctant Vegetarians and Terra Novian Reports, to name a few. He and his wife (and oft times co-author), Vicky, have been married since 1988 and divide their time between Ontario, Canada and the island of Eleuthera in The Bahamas.

Find all of Geoff's books at

https://ebooks.geezerguides.com

Follow Geoff on social media

 https://facebook.com/AuthorGeoffWells/

 geoffwells@ebooks.geezerguides.com

About Our Cookbooks

Quality

We are passionate about producing quality cookbooks. You'll never find "cut and pasted" recipes in any of our books.

Consistency

We endeavor to create consistent methods for both ingredients and instructions. In most of our recipes, the ingredients will be listed in the order in which they are used. We also try to make sure that the instructions make sense, are clear and are arranged in a logical order.

Only Quality Ingredients

To ensure that all of our recipes turn out exactly right, we call for only fresh, quality ingredients. You'll never find "ingredients" such as cake mixes, artificial sweeteners, artificial egg replacements, or any pre-packaged items. Ingredients, to us, are items in their natural (or as close to natural as possible), singular form: eggs, milk, cream, flour, salt, sugar, butter, coconut oil, vanilla extract, etc.

English Speaking Authors

We write all our books ourselves and never outsource them or scrape content from the Internet.

 ## Found an Error?

Although we do our best to make sure everything is accurate and complete, mistakes happen.

If you've found an error - a missing ingredient, an incorrect measurement, a temperature that's wrong, etc. - please let us know so we can correct it.

Just e-mail us at oops@geezerguides.com and we'll make any necessary corrections.

Published by Geezer Guides

When you see *Published by Geezer Guides* on any book, you can be confident that you are purchasing a quality product.

About Geezer Guides

Geezer Guides is a small independent publisher that only publishes original manuscripts. We will never sell you something that has just been copied from the Internet. All our books are properly formatted with a clickable table of contents.

Other Books You May Like

You can find our complete catalog at

https://ebooks.geezerguides.com

Plus Many More

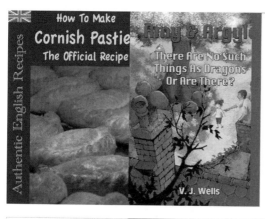

Made in the USA
Middletown, DE
11 December 2020

27373605R00113